The Supporters' Guide to Premier & Football League Clubs 1999

EDITOR
John Robinson

Fifteenth Edition

British Library Cataloguing in Publication Data
A catalogue record for this book is available from the British Library

ISBN 1-86223-019-6

Printed by The Cromwell Press

FOREWORD

We are indebted to the staffs of the clubs featured in this guide for their cooperation and also to Michael Robinson (page layouts), Bob Budd (cover artwork) and Owen Pavey and Kevin Norminton (photos).

When using this guide, please note that 'child' concessions generally include senior citizens also. A number of clubs had not set their 1998/99 Season admission prices when we completed the guide and where this was the case we have shown 1997/98 price information.

Similarly, the price of programmes may change for some clubs for, or during, the 1998/99 season and we have included the latest information available.

At the time of our going to print, Brighton and Hove Albion's application to move back to play their games in Brighton had still to be approved by the Football League. We have, therefore, again included the travelling information for the Priestfield Stadium, but have illustrated it with a picture of the Withdene Stadium!

Disabled Supporters' information is once again included in the guide and, to ensure that facilities are not overstretched, we recommend that disabled fans pre-book wherever possible.

Regular purchasers of the guide will notice that we have used many new ground photos to illustrate the incredible developments which have taken place over the last 3 or 4 years. However, ground moves and redevelopment are continuing apace and travelling fans may find that away sections and prices change during the course of the 1998/99 season.

Finally, we would like to wish our readers a happy and safe spectating season.

John Robinson
EDITOR

CONTENTS

WEMBLEY STADIUM

Opened: 1923	**Record Attendance**: 100,000
Location: Wembley, Middlesex HA9 0DW	**Pitch Size**: 115 × 75 yards
Telephone: Box Office (0181) 900-1234	**Ground Capacity**: 80,000
Telephone: Admin. (0181) 902-8833	**Seating Capacity**: 80,000
FAX Number: (0181) 903-4818	

(PLAYERS TUNNEL END)
EAST TERRACE

OLYMPIC WAY & TWIN TOWERS (ROYAL BOX SIDE)

SOUTH STAND

WEST TERRACE
(STADIUM OFFICE END)

GENERAL INFORMATION
Guided Tours Available: (0181) 902-8833
(extension 3346) for details
Car Parking: Car park for over 7,000 vehicles
Coach Parking: Car park at Stadium
Nearest Railway Stations: Wembley Park, Wembley
Central, Wembley Complex (5-10 minutes walk)
Nearest Police Station: Mobile Unit in front of
Twin Towers
Police Telephone Nº: (0181) 903-4818

GROUND INFORMATION
Location of Family Area: North Stand

DISABLED INFORMATION
Wheelchairs: Limited facilities available
Disabled Toilets: Yes

ADMISSION INFO (1998/99 PRICES)
Admission £14.00 – £36.00; depending on the game
and ground position. Also a £1 per seat booking fee
(**Accompanied Children – half-price in family
enclosure**)

How to get to Wembley By Road

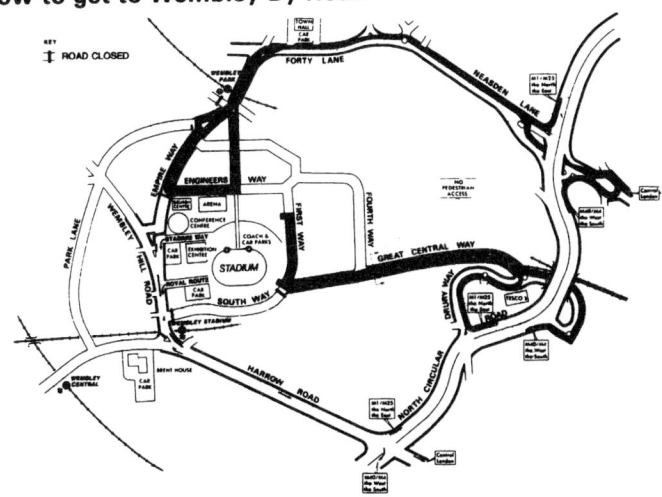

The F.A. Carling Premiership

Founded
1992

Address
16 Lancaster Gate, London   W2 3LW

Phone
(0171) 402-7151

The Nationwide Football League

Founded
1888

Address
Lytham St. Annes, Lancashire   FY8 1JG

Phone
(01253) 729421

ARSENAL FC

Founded: 1886 (**Entered League:** 1893)	**Colours:** Shirts – Red with White Sleeves
Former Names: Royal Arsenal (1886-91);	Shorts – White
Woolwich Arsenal (1891-1914)	**Telephone Nº:** (0171) 704-4000
Nickname: 'Gunners'	**Ticket Office:** (0171) 704-4040
Ground: Arsenal Stadium, Avenell Road,	**Fax Number:** (0171) 704-4001
Highbury, London N5 1BU	**Pitch Size:** 110×71 yards
Record Attendance: 73,295 (9/3/35)	**Ground Capacity:** 38,300 (All seats)

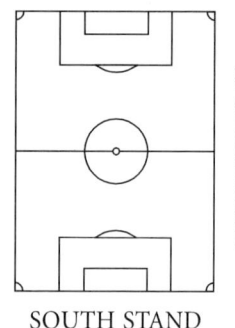

(GILLESPIE ROAD)
NORTH BANK STAND

WEST STAND
Highbury Hill Turnstiles

EAST STAND
AVENELL ROAD

SOUTH STAND

GENERAL INFORMATION

Supporters Club: c/o Barry Baker, 154 St. Thomas's Road, Finsbury Park, London N4
Telephone Nº: (0171) 226-1627
Car Parking: Street Parking
Coach Parking: Drayton Park (N5)
Nearest Railway Stat'n: Drayton Park/Finsbury Park
Nearest Tube Station: Arsenal (Piccadilly)
Club Shop: At ground and at Finsbury Park Tube
Opening Times: Weekdays 9.30am to 5.00pm; Saturday Matchdays 1.00pm onwards
Telephone Nº: (0171) 704-4120
Postal Sales: Yes
Nearest Police Stat'n: 284 Hornsey Road, Holloway
Police Telephone Nº: (0171) 263-9090

GROUND INFORMATION

Away Supporters' Entrances & Sections:
South Stand – Blocks 17 & 18

ADMISSION INFO (1998/99 PRICES)

Adult Seating: £14.00 – £34.00
Child Seating: £8.00 (members only, Family Stand)
Programme Price: £2.00

DISABLED INFORMATION

Wheelchairs: 95 spaces in total for Home and Away fans in the disabled section, Lower Tier East Stand
Helpers: One helper admitted per wheelchair
Prices: Free of charge for Disabled and Helpers
Disabled Toilets: 3 Available in the South Stand, one available in the Lower East 'H' Block
Commentaries are available for the blind
Are Bookings Necessary: Yes
Contact: (0171) 704-4000

Travelling Supporters' Information:
Routes: From North: Exit M1 at Junction 2 following City signs. After Holloway Road Station (6¼ miles) 3rd left into Drayton Park, after ¾ mile right into Aubert Park and 2nd left into Avenell Road. From South: From London Bridge follow signs to Bank of England then Angel. Right at traffic lights to Highbury Roundabout (1 mile), into Holloway Road then 3rd right into Drayton Park (then as North). From West: Exit M4 Junction 1 towards Chiswick (A315), left after 1 mile (A40) to M41 then A40(M) to A501 Ring Road turn left Angel to Highbury Roundabout (then as South).

Aston Villa FC

Founded: 1874 (**Entered League**: 1888)	**Colours**: Shirts – Claret and Blue
Former Names: None	Shorts – White
Nickname: 'The Villans' 'Villa'	**Telephone Nº**: (0121) 327-2299
Ground: Villa Park, Trinity Road,	**Ticket Office**: (0121) 327-5353
Birmingham B6 6HE	**Fax Number**: (0121) 322-2107
Record Attendance: 76,588 (2/3/46)	**Pitch Size**: 115 × 75 yards
	Ground Capacity: 39,372 (All seats)

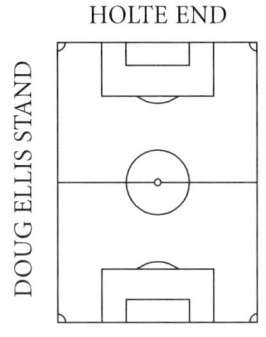

HOLTE END
DOUG ELLIS STAND
TRINITY ROAD STAND & ENCLOSURE
NORTH STAND
WITTON END

GENERAL INFORMATION

Supporters Club: Special Projects Office
Telephone Nº: (0121) 327-2299
Car Parking: Aston Villa Leisure Centre Car Park, Aston Hall Road. Also at the Siemens Site, Brookvale Road, Witton
Away Coach Parking: Opposite the ground
Nearest Railway Station: Witton or Aston (5 mins. walk)
Nearest Bus Station: Birmingham Centre
Club Shop: 'Villa Village' – at the ground
Opening Times: Weekdays and Matchdays 9.30am to 5.00pm (closes during the match)
Telephone Nº: (0121) 327-2800
Postal Sales: Yes
Nearest Police Stat'n: Queen's Road, Aston (½ mile)
Police Telephone Nº: (0121) 322-6010

GROUND INFORMATION

Away Supporters' Entrances & Sections:
Witton End – 'R' Block

ADMISSION INFO (1998/99 PRICES)

Adult Seating: £17.00 – £22.00
Child Seating: £8.50 – £11.00
Programme Price: £2.00

DISABLED INFORMATION

Wheelchairs: 56 spaces in total for Home and Away fans in a special section – Trinity Road Stand & Holte End
Helpers: By letter of request of disabled – One per disabled fan
Prices: At club's discretion for the disabled. Helpers full price
Disabled Toilets: Trinity Road Stand & Holte End Commentaries are available by arrangement
Are Bookings Necessary: Yes
Contact: (0121) 327-5353

Travelling Supporters' Information:
Routes: From all parts: Exit M6 at Junction 6 (Spaghetti Junction). Follow signs for Birmingham (NE). Take the 4th exit at the roundabout onto the A38 (M) signposted Aston. After ½ mile, turn right into Aston Hall Road.
Bus Services: Service 7 from Bull Street to Witton Square. Also some specials.

BARNET FC

Founded: 1888 (**Entered League**: 1991)	**Colours**: Shirts – Amber w/ Black Panel
Former Names: Barnet Alston FC	Shorts – Black w/ Amber Trim
Nickname: 'Bees'	**Telephone Nº**: (0181) 441-6932
Ground: Underhill Stadium, Barnet	**Ticket Office**: (0181) 449-6325
Lane, Barnet, Herts. EN5 2BE	**Fax Number**: (0181) 447-0655
Record Attendance: 11,026 (1952)	**Ground Capacity**: 4,015
Pitch Size: 113 × 72 yards	**Seating Capacity**: 1,902

SOUTH STAND
(Away)

PRIORY GROVE

EAST TERRACE

BARNET LANE
MAIN STAND

NORTH TERRACE

GENERAL INFORMATION

Supporters Club: c/o Club Shop
Telephone Nº: (0181) 440-0725
Car Parking: Street Parking and High Barnet Underground Car Park
Coach Parking: By Police Direction
Nearest Railway Stat'n: New Barnet (1½ miles)
Nearest Tube Station: High Barnet (Northern) (5 minutes walk)
Club Shop: 40 High Street, Barnet
Opening Times: Monday to Saturday 10.00am to 6.00pm
Telephone Nº: (0181) 441-6932
Postal Sales: Yes
Nearest Police Station: Barnet (¼ mile)
Police Telephone Nº: (0181) 200-2212

GROUND INFORMATION

Away Supporters' Entrances & Sections:
Entrances in Priory Grove for the South Stand

ADMISSION INFO (1998/99 PRICES)

Adult Standing: £8.00 (Members £6.00 North Tce.)
Adult Seating: £14.00 (£10.00 in the Family Stand)
Child Standing: £4.00 (Members free North Tce.)
Child Seating: £7.00 (£5.00 in the Family Stand)
(Family Tickets are also available)
Programme Price: £1.50
Note: Concessionary prices are for members only

DISABLED INFORMATION

Wheelchairs: 12 spaces in total for Home and Away fans in the Family Stand – Barnet Lane Entrance
Helpers: One helper admitted per wheelchair
Prices: £8.00 in the Family Stand
Disabled Toilets: One available in the Social Club
Are Bookings Necessary: Yes
Contact: (0181) 441-6932

Travelling Supporters' Information:
Routes: The ground is situated off the Great North Road (A1000) at the foot of Barnet Hill near to the junction with Station Road (A110). Barnet Lane is on the west of the A1000 next to the Cricket Ground.

BARNSLEY FC

Founded: 1887 **(Entered League:** 1898)	**Colours:** Shirts – Red
Former Names: Barnsley St. Peter's	Shorts – White
Nickname: 'Tykes' 'Colliers' 'Reds'	**Telephone Nº:** (01226) 211211
Ground: Oakwell Ground, Grove Street,	**Ticket Office:** (01226) 211211
Barnsley S71 1ET	**Fax Number:** (01226) 211444
Record Attendance: 40,255 (15/2/36)	**Pitch Size:** 110 × 75 yards
	Ground Capacity: 19,020 (All seats)

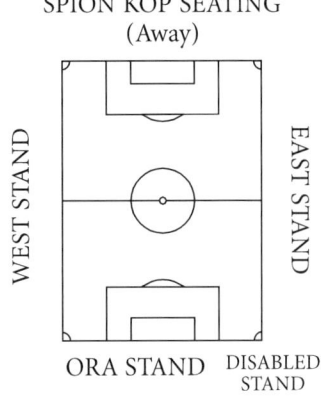

SPION KOP SEATING (Away)

WEST STAND · EAST STAND · ORA STAND · DISABLED STAND

GENERAL INFORMATION

Supporters Club: Mr. A. Bloore, c/o Barnsley FC
Telephone Nº: (01302) 883481
Car Parking: Queen's Ground Car Park (adjacent)
Coach Parking: Queen's Ground Car Park
Nearest Railway Stat'n: Barnsley Exchange (5 mins. walk)
Nearest Bus Station: Barnsley Exchange
Club Shop: Large shop at ground
Opening Times: Monday to Saturday 9.00am to 5.00pm. Saturday Matchdays open until 5.30pm. Evening matches open until 10.15pm
Telephone Nº: (01226) 211211
Postal Sales: Yes (Also Credit Card Sales)
Nearest Police Station: Churchfields, Barnsley
Police Telephone Nº: (0114) 220-2020

GROUND INFORMATION

Away Supporters' Entrances & Sections:
Spion Kop Stand, Entrances 41 to 47

ADMISSION INFO (1998/99 PRICES)

Adult Seating: See below
Child Seating: See below
Note: At the time of going to press, the availability and price of matchday tickets for away fans was not known.
Programme Price: £2.00

DISABLED INFORMATION

Wheelchairs: A new disabled stand is expected to be opened during the season and will provide accommodation to those in wheelchairs and blind supporters.
Helpers: Admitted depending on room available
Prices: £10.00 for the disabled and for helpers. Alternatively, a limited number of Pre-booked places are available in the disabled section of the Ora Stand
Disabled Toilets: Adjacent to the Disabled Stand Commentaries are available for the blind
Are Bookings Necessary: Yes
Contact: (01226) 211211

Travelling Supporters' Information:
Routes: From All Parts: Exit the M1 at Junction 37 and follow the 'Barnsley FC/Football Ground' signs which lead to a large surface car park adjacent to the ground (2 miles).

BIRMINGHAM CITY FC

Founded: 1875 (**Entered League**: 1892)
Former Names: Small Heath Alliance FC
(1875-88); Small Heath FC (1888-1905);
Birmingham FC (1905-1945)
Nickname: 'Blues'
Ground: St. Andrew's Stadium,
Birmingham   B9 4NH
Record Attendance: 68,844 (11/2/39)

Colours: Shirts – Blue
        Shorts – White
Telephone Nº: (0121) 772-0101
Ticket Office: (0121) 772-0101
Fax Number: (0121) 766-7866
Pitch Size: 115 × 75 yards
Ground Capacity: 20,000 approximately
until February 1999 when the capacity
will be increased to 30,200 (all seats)

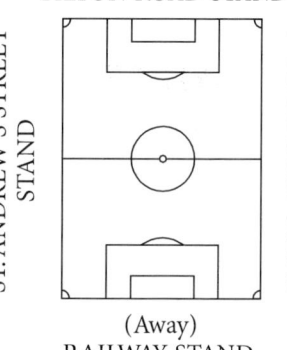

TILTON ROAD STAND

ST. ANDREW'S STREET STAND

CATTELL ROAD STAND

(Away)
RAILWAY STAND

GENERAL INFORMATION

Supporters Club: c/o Linda Goodman,
69 Malmesbury Road, Small Heath, Birmingham
Telephone Nº: (0121) 773-5088
Car Parking: Street Parking
Coach Parking: Coventry Road
Nearest Railway Stat'n: Birmingham New Street or
Birmingham Moor Street (20 minutes walk)
Nearest Bus Station: Digbeth
Club Shops: At Dale End & Cattell Road Superstore
Opening Times: Monday to Saturday 9.00am to
5.30pm
Telephone Nº: (0121) 212-0873 + (0121) 772-0101
Postal Sales: Yes
Nearest Police Station: Bordesley Green (½ mile)
Police Telephone Nº: (0121) 772-1166

GROUND INFORMATION

Away Supporters' Entrances & Sections:
Railway Stand End

ADMISSION INFO (1998/99 PRICES)

Adult Seating: £11.50 – £20.00
Child Seating: £6.50 – £9.00
Note: Prices vary according to match category and
the position in the ground
Programme Price: £1.70

DISABLED INFORMATION

Wheelchairs: Spaces available in the Cattell Road
Stand and Family Stand.
Helpers: One helper admitted per wheelchair
Prices: £5.00 for disabled fans, £7.00 for helpers
Disabled Toilets: Available in the Cattell Road and
Family Stands
Are Bookings Necessary: Yes
Contact: (0121) 772-0101

Travelling Supporters' Information:
Routes: From All Parts: Exit M6 at Junction 6 and take the A38 (M) (Aston Expressway). Leave at 2nd exit then
take first exit at roundabout along the Dartmouth Middleway. After 1¼ miles turn left into St. Andrew's Street.
Bus Services: Services 96 & 97 from Birmingham; Services 98 & 99 from Digbeth.

BLACKBURN ROVERS FC

Founded: 1875 (**Entered League**: 1888) **Former Names**: None **Nickname**: 'Rovers' 'Blues & Whites' **Ground**: Ewood Park, Blackburn, Lancashire BB2 4JF **Record Attendance**: 61,783 (2/3/29)	**Colours**: Shirts – Blue and White Halves Shorts – White **Telephone Nº**: (01254) 698888 **Ticket Office**: (01321) 101010 **Fax Number**: (01254) 671042 **Pitch Size**: 117 × 73 yards **Ground Capacity**: 31,169 (All seats)

DARWEN END
(Away)

WALKERSTEEL STAND

JACK WALKER STAND

BOLTON ROAD

BLACKBURN END
KIDDER STREET

GENERAL INFORMATION
Supporters Club: Barbara Magee, c/o Ewood Park
Telephone Nº: (01254) 698888
Car Parking: Street Parking (nearby)
Coach Parking: By Police direction
Nearest Railway Stat'n: Blackburn Central (1½ mls)
Nearest Bus Station: Blackburn Central (1½ miles)
Club Shop: At Ground
Opening Times: Weekdays 9.00am to 5.30pm;
Saturday Matchdays 9.30am to 3.00pm; Sundays
11.00am to 3.00pm
Telephone Nº: (01254) 672333
Postal Sales: Yes
Nearest Police Station: Blackburn (2 miles)
Police Telephone Nº: (01254) 51212

GROUND INFORMATION
Away Supporters' Entrances & Sections:
Darwen End

ADMISSION INFO (1998/99 PRICES)
Adult Seating: £18.00 – £28.00 (Price depends on category of game)
Child Seating: £10.00
Programme Price: £1.50

DISABLED INFORMATION
Wheelchairs: 140 spaces in total for Home and Away fans in the disabled section, Walkersteel Stand
Helpers: One helper admitted per disabled fan
Prices: Free for the Disabled. Helpers normal prices
Disabled Toilets: Available in the disabled section
Commentaries are available by arrangement for up to 6 people
Are Bookings Necessary: Yes
Contact: (01254) 698888

Travelling Supporters' Information:
Routes: From North & South: Exit M6 at Junction 31, take A59/A677 towards Blackburn. After 1½ miles, the road splits – stay on A677. After approx. 5 miles turn right at Esso Garage onto Montague Street, cross over King Street into Byron Street, left into Canterbury Street and follow one-way system until T-junction with the Bolton Road A666. Turn right for Ewood Park; From the South-East: Exit M61 at Junction 8 onto A674. After 5 miles turn right onto A6062 for 3 miles until the Bolton Road A666. Turn right and Ewood Park is ¼ mile on left; From the East: Exit M65 at Junction 6, turn left onto A6119 Whitebirk Road for ½ mile, turn right onto A677 for ½ mile and bear left onto the A679 for 1 mile. Turn left onto A666 for 1¼ miles and Ewood Park is on the left.

BLACKPOOL FC

Founded: 1887 (**Entered League:** 1896) **Former Names:** Merged with Blackpool St. Johns in 1887 **Nickname:** 'Seasiders' **Ground:** Bloomfield Road, Blackpool, Lancashire FY1 6JJ **Record Attendance:** 38,098 (17/9/55)	**Colours:** Shirts – Tangerine Shorts – Tangerine **Telephone Nº:** (01253) 405331 **Ticket Office:** (01253) 404331 **Fax Number:** (01253) 405011 **Pitch Size:** 112 × 74 yards **Ground Capacity:** 11,295 **Seating Capacity:** 3,041

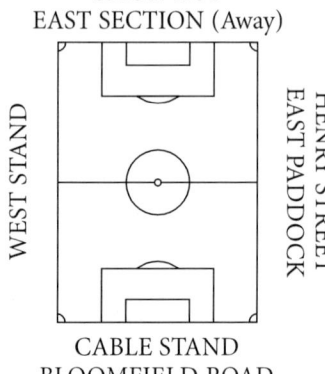

SPION KOP
EAST SECTION (Away)

WEST STAND

HENRY STREET
EAST PADDOCK

CABLE STAND
BLOOMFIELD ROAD

GENERAL INFORMATION

Supporters Club: c/o Club
Telephone Nº: (01253) 405331
Car Parking: Car Park at the Ground for 3,000 cars and street parking
Coach Parking: Mecca Car Park (behind Spion Kop)
Nearest Railway Stat'n: Blackpool South (5 mins.)
Nearest Bus Station: Talbot Road (2 miles)
Club Shop: At Ground and at Edward Street
Opening Times: Daily from 9.00am to 5.15pm
Telephone Nº: (01253) 405331 + (01253) 752222
Postal Sales: Yes
Nearest Police Station: South Shore, Montague Street, Blackpool
Police Telephone Nº: (01253) 293933

GROUND INFORMATION

Away Supporters' Entrances & Sections:
Spion Kop turnstiles for the Spion Kop and East Paddock North Section

ADMISSION INFO (1998/99 PRICES)

Adult Standing: £10.00
Adult Seating: £12.00 – £13.00
Child Standing: £5.00 (£7.00 for away supporters)
Child Seating: £6.50 – £7.50
FAMILY BLOCK: – Various additional discounts available to home supporters only
1 Adult + 1 Child   £15.00
2 Adults + 1 Child   £27.00
Programme Price: £1.70

DISABLED INFORMATION

Wheelchairs: 13 spaces in total for Home and Away fans in the disabled area, South Stand
Helpers: One helper admitted per disabled fan
Prices: Free of charge for Disabled. £10 for Helpers
Disabled Toilets: None
Are Bookings Necessary: Yes
Contact: (01253) 405331

Travelling Supporters' Information:
Routes: From All Parts: Exit M6 at Junction 32 onto the M55. Follow signs for the main car parks along the new 'spine' road to the car parks at the side of the ground.

BOLTON WANDERERS FC

Founded: 1874 (**Entered League:** 1888) **Former Names:** Christchurch FC (1874-1877) **Nickname:** 'Trotters' **Ground:** Reebok Stadium, Lostock, Bolton, Lancashire **Record Attendance:** 25,000	**Colours:** Shirts – White Shorts – Blue **Telephone Nº:** (01204) 673673 **Ticket Office:** (01204) 673600 **Fax Number:** (01204) 673773 **Pitch Size:** 114 × 74 yards **Ground Capacity:** 25,000 (All seats)

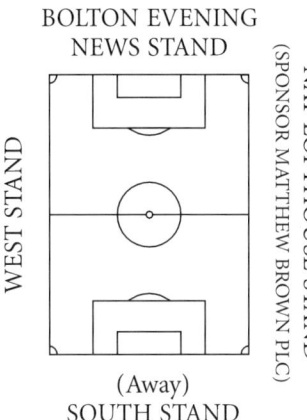

BOLTON EVENING NEWS STAND

WEST STAND

NAT LOFTHOUSE STAND (SPONSOR MATTHEW BROWN PLC)

(Away)
SOUTH STAND

GENERAL INFORMATION

Supporters Club: c/o P. Entwistle, 21 Woodfield, Bolton
Telephone Nº: –
Car Parking: 2,800 spaces at the ground
Coach Parking: At the ground
Nearest Railway Station: Bolton Trinity Street (4 miles)
Nearest Bus Station: Moor Lane, Bolton
Club Shop: At the ground
Opening Times: Daily from 9.30am to 5.30pm
Telephone Nº: (01204) 673650
Postal Sales: Yes
Nearest Police Station: Howell Croft, Bolton
Police Telephone Nº: (01204) 522466

GROUND INFORMATION

Away Supporters' Entrances & Sections:
South Stand entrances and accommodation

ADMISSION INFO (1998/99 PRICES)

Adult Seating: £14.00 – £19.00
Child Seating: £9.00 – £11.00
Programme Price: £2.00

DISABLED INFORMATION

Wheelchairs: 32 spaces available for visiting fans, 72 spaces for home fans
Helpers: One helper admitted per disabled fan
Prices: Free for wheelchair users. Helpers normal prices
Disabled Toilets: Yes
Are Bookings Necessary: Yes
Contact: (01204) 673673

Travelling Supporters' Information:
Routes: From All Parts: Exit the M61 at Junction 6 and the ground is clearly visible ¼ mile away.

AFC BOURNEMOUTH

Founded: 1899 (**Entered League**: 1923)
Former Names: Boscombe FC (1899-1923); Bournemouth & Boscombe Athletic FC (1923-1972)
Nickname: 'Cherries'
Ground: Dean Court, Bournemouth, Dorset BH7 7AF
Record Attendance: 28,799 (2/3/57)

Colours: Shirts – Red & Black Stripes
Shorts – Black
Telephone Nº: (01202) 395381
Ticket Office: (01202) 395381
Fax Number: (01202) 309797
Pitch Size: 112 × 74 yards
Ground Capacity: 10,770
Seating Capacity: 3,141

KINGS PARK
SOUTH STAND

CAR PARK (Away) MAIN STAND

THISTLEBARROW ROAD
NEW STAND

BRIGHTON BEACH
TERRACE (Away)

GENERAL INFORMATION

Supporters Club: c/o Dean Court Supporters' Club, Bournemouth BH7 7AF
Telephone Nº: (01202) 398313
Car Parking: Car Park for 1,500 cars behind Main Stand
Coach Parking: Kings Park (nearby)
Nearest Railway Station: Bournemouth Central (1½ ml)
Nearest Bus Station: Holdenhurst Road, Bournemouth
Club Shop: At Ground
Opening Times: Weekdays 10.00am to 4.30pm; Saturday Matchdays 12.30pm to kick-off
Telephone Nº: (01202) 397777/395381
Postal Sales: Yes
Nearest Police Station: Boscombe (400 yards)
Police Telephone Nº: (01202) 552099

GROUND INFORMATION

Away Supporters' Entrances & Sections:
Main Stand Turnstiles (Block A) for Brighton Beach Terrace (open)

ADMISSION INFO (1998/99 PRICES)

Adult Standing: £8.50 – £10.00
Adult Seating: £10.50 – £15.00
Child Standing: £5.00
Child Seating: £4.00 – £9.00
Programme Price: £1.60

DISABLED INFORMATION

Wheelchairs: 16 spaces in total for Home and Away fans in the disabled section, South Stand
Helpers: One helper admitted per disabled fan
Prices: Free of charge for Disabled and Helpers
Disabled Toilets: Available adjacent to South Stand
Are Bookings Necessary: Yes
Contact: (01202) 395381

Travelling Supporters' Information:
Routes: From North & East: Take A338 into Bournemouth and turn left at 'Kings Park' turning. Then first left at mini-roundabout and first right into Thistlebarrow Road for ground; From West: Use A3049, turning right at Wallisdown Roundabout to Talbot Roundabout. Take first exit at Talbot Roundabout (over Wessex Way), then left at mini-roundabout. Go straight on at traffic lights then right at mini-roundabout into Kings Park for ground.

BRADFORD CITY FC

Founded: 1903 (**Entered League**: 1903)	**Colours**: Shirts – Claret & Amber
Former Names: None	Shorts – Black
Nickname: 'Bantams'	**Telephone Nº**: (01274) 773355
Ground: Valley Parade, Bradford	**Ticket Office**: (01274) 770022
BD8 7DY	**Fax Number**: (01274) 773356
Record Attendance: 39,146 (11/3/11)	**Ground Capacity**: 18,000
Pitch Size: 110 × 80 yards	**Seating Capacity**: 11,500

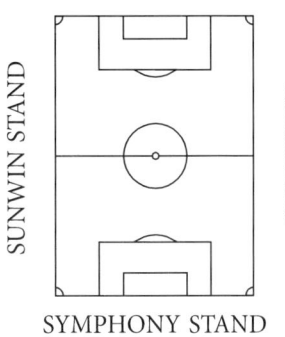

DIAMOND SEAL KOP

SUNWIN STAND

CIBA STAND

SYMPHONY STAND

GENERAL INFORMATION

Supporters Club: c/o Philip Ideson, 66 Clayton Hall Road, Crosshills, Keighley   BD20 7TB
Telephone Nº: (01535) 631076
Car Parking: Street Parking and Car Parks (£2.50 entry charge)
Coach Parking: By Police direction
Nearest Railway Station: Bradford Interchange
Nearest Bus Station: Bradford Interchange (1 mile)
Club Shop: At Ground
Opening Times: Monday to Saturday 9.00-5.00
Telephone Nº: (01274) 770012
Postal Sales: Yes
Nearest Police Station: Tyrrells, Bradford
Police Telephone Nº: (01274) 723422

GROUND INFORMATION

Away Supporters' Entrances & Sections:
Symphony Stand entrances and accommodation

ADMISSION INFO (1998/99 PRICES)

Adult Standing: £9.00
Adult Seating: £13.00
Child Standing: £5.00
Child Seating: £7.00
Note: Special concessions available in Family Stand
Programme Price: £1.80

DISABLED INFORMATION

Wheelchairs: 49 spaces in total for Home and Away fans in the disabled area, 'A' Block of the Sunwin Stand and also in the CIBA Stand
Helpers: One helper admitted per disabled fan
Prices: Half-price for disabled fans and helpers
Disabled Toilets: Available behind the disabled area
Are Bookings Necessary: Yes
Contact: (01274) 770022

Travelling Supporters' Information:
Routes: Exit the M62 at Junction 26 and take the M606 towards Bradford. At the end of the motorway, take the last exit into Rooley Lane (signs for the Airport). A McDonalds is now on your left. At the second roundabout, turn left into Wakefield Road and stay in the middle lane. Staying in the middle lane, continue straight on over two roundabouts (signs to Skipley and Skipton) onto Shipley Airedale Road which then becomes Canal Road. Just after the Staples Office Equipment showroom on the left, turn left into Station Road and left again into Queens Road. Go up the hill to the second set of traffic lights and turn left into Manningham Lane. After the SAVE petrol station on the left, turn first left into Valley Parade for the Stadium.

BRENTFORD FC

Founded: 1889 (**Entered League:** 1920)
Former Names: None
Nickname: 'Bees'
Ground: Griffin Park, Braemar Road, Brentford, Middlesex TW8 0NT
Record Attendance: 38,678 (26/2/49)
Pitch Size: 111 × 74 yards

Colours: Shirts – Red and White Stripes
Shorts – Black
Telephone Nº: (0181) 847-2511
Ticket Office: (0181) 847-2511
Fax Number: (0181) 568-9940
Ground Capacity: 12,763
Seating Capacity: 8,920

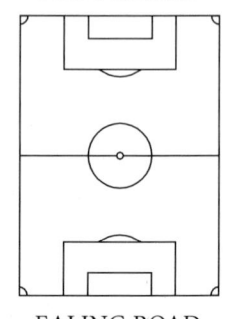

SEATS & TERRACING
BROOK ROAD

BRAEMAR ROAD
MAIN STAND

NEW ROAD
STAND

EALING ROAD
TERRACING

GENERAL INFORMATION

Supporters Club: c/o Mr P. Gilham, 16 Hartland Road, Hampton Hill, Middlesex
Telephone Nº: (0181) 941-0425
Car Parking: Street Parking
Coach Parking: Leyton Road Car Park
Nearest Railway Stat'n: Brentford Central (½ mile)
Nearest Tube Station: South Ealing (Piccadilly) (1 mile)
Club Shop: At Ground
Opening Times: Weekdays and matchdays 11.00am to 5.00pm. Closed between 2 & 3pm for lunch
Telephone Nº: (0181) 560-9836
Postal Sales: Yes
Nearest Police Station: Brentford
Police Telephone Nº: (0181) 569-9728

GROUND INFORMATION

Away Supporters' Entrances & Sections:
Brook Road

ADMISSION INFO (1998/99 PRICES)

Adult Standing: £8.00
Adult Seating: £9.00 – £15.00
Child Standing: £5.00
Child Seating: £6.00 – £12.00
Programme Price: £1.50

DISABLED INFORMATION

Wheelchairs: 9 spaces in total for Home and Away fans in the disabled section, Braemar Road
Helpers: One helper admitted per disabled fan
Prices: Free of charge for Disabled and Helpers
Disabled Toilets: Available in the disabled section
Commentaries are available for the blind
Are Bookings Necessary: Yes
Contact: (0181) 560-6062

Travelling Supporters' Information:
Routes: From North: Take the A406 North Circular (from the M1/A1) to the Chiswick Roundabout and then along the Great West Road and turn left at the third set of traffic lights into Ealing Road; From East: Take the A406 to the Chiswick Roundabout, then as North; From West: Exit M4 at Junction 2 – down to the Chiswick Roundabout, then as North; From South: Use the A3, M3, A240 or A316 to Kew Road, continue along over Kew Bridge, turn left at the traffic lights, then right at the next traffic lights into Ealing Road.

Brighton & Hove Albion FC

Founded: 1900 (**Entered League**: 1920)
Former Names: Brighton & Hove
Rangers FC (1900-1901)
Nickname: 'Seagulls'
Office: 118 Queen's Road, Brighton,
East Sussex   BN1 3XG
Note: For the 1998/99 Season, Brighton will be
groundsharing with Gillingham FC until
October & thereafter hope to move to Withdene

Stadium (pictured), Tong Dene Lane, Brighton
Colours: Shirts – Blue and White Stripes
Shorts – Blue
Telephone Nº: (01273) 778855
Ticket Office: (01273) 778855
Fax Number: (01273) 321095
Pitch Size: 114 × 75 yards
Ground Capacity: Approximately 9,000
Seating Capacity: 3,590

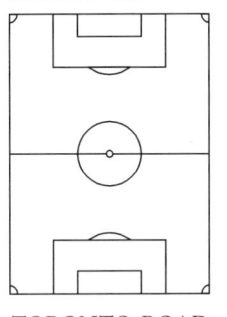

PRIESTFIELD ROAD
GILLINGHAM END

GORDON ROAD STAND

REDFERN AVENUE
MAINSTAND

TORONTO ROAD
RAINHAM END

GENERAL INFORMATION

Supporters Club: c/o Liz Costa, 72 Stoneham
Road, Hove   BN3 5HH
Telephone Nº: (01273) 885658
Car Parking: Street Parking
Coach Parking: By Police direction
Nearest Railway Station: Gillingham
Nearest Bus Station: Gillingham
Club Shop: 6 Queen's Road, Brighton
Opening Times: Monday to Saturday 10.00am –
5.00pm
Telephone Nº: (01273) 778855
Postal Sales: Yes
Nearest Police Station: Gillingham
Police Telephone Nº: (01634) 234488

GROUND INFORMATION

Away Supporters' Entrances & Sections:
Redfern Avenue turnstiles for Redfern Avenue
Corner (Gillingham End)

ADMISSION INFO (1998/99 PRICES)

Adult Standing: £8.00
Adult Seating: £10.00 – £12.00
Child Standing: £4.00
Child Seating: £5.00 – £6.00
Programme Price: £1.50

DISABLED INFORMATION

Wheelchairs: 20 spaces in total for Home and Away
fans in the disabled section, adjacent to Main Stand
Helpers: One helper admitted per disabled person
Prices: Free for the disabled. Helpers normal prices
Disabled Toilets: None
Are Bookings Necessary: Preferred
Contact: (01634) 851462

FOR DIRECTIONS TO THE WITHDENE
STADIUM, PLEASE CONTACT THE
CLUB AT THE OFFICE ADDRESS

Travelling Supporters' Information:
Routes: From All Parts: Exit M2 at Junction 4 and follow the link road (dual carriageway) B278 to the 3rd rounda-
bout. Turn left onto the A2 (dual carriageway) and go across the roundabout to the traffic lights. Turn right into
Woodlands Road after the traffic lights. The ground is ¼ mile on the left.

BRISTOL CITY FC

Founded: 1894 (**Entered League:** 1901)	**Colours:** Shirts – Red
Former Names: Bristol South End FC	Shorts – White
(1894-1897)	**Telephone Nº:** (0117) 963-0630
Nickname: 'Robins'	**Ticket Hotline:** (0117) 966-6666
Ground: Ashton Gate, Bristol BS3 2EJ	**Fax Number:** (0117) 963-0700
Record Attendance: 43,335 (16/2/35)	**Pitch Size:** 115 × 75 yards
	Ground Capacity: 21,497 (All seats)

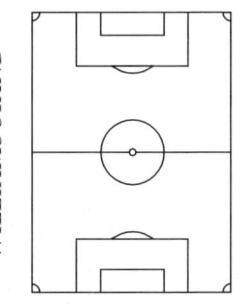

CARLING ATYEO STAND

BRUNEL FORD WILLIAMS STAND

EVENING POST DOLMAN STAND

DATABASE COMPUTERS
WEDLOCK STAND (Away)
(CAR PARK)

GENERAL INFORMATION
Supporters Club: Mr Richard Davies, c/o Club
Telephone Nº: (0117) 966-5554
Car Parking: Street Parking
Coach Parking: Winterstoke Road
Nearest Railway Station: Bristol Temple Meads (1½ miles)
Nearest Bus Station: Bristol City Centre
Club Shop: At the ground
Opening Times: Weekdays 9.00am to 5.30pm and Saturdays 9.30am to 12.00pm
Telephone Nº: (0117) 963-0637 & (0117) 963-0666
Postal Sales: Yes
Nearest Police Station: Kings Mead Lane (2 miles) – Office at ground
Police Telephone Nº: (0117) 927-7777

GROUND INFORMATION
Away Supporters' Entrances & Sections:
Database Computers Wedlock Stand

ADMISSION INFO (1998/99 PRICES)
Adult Seating: £13.00 – £23.00
Child Seating: £5.00 – £12.00
Note: Membership discounts are available and prices vary according to the category of the game
Programme Price: £1.80

DISABLED INFORMATION
Wheelchairs: Limited number accommodated at Pitchside – please apply early
Helpers: One helper admitted per disabled fan
Prices: Free for the disabled. Helpers normal price
Disabled Toilets: 2 available
Commentaries are available for the blind (contact the club for further information)
Are Bookings Necessary: Yes
Contact: (0117) 963-0630

Travelling Supporters' Information:
Routes: From North & West: Exit M5 at Junction 16, take the A38 to Bristol City Centre and follow the A38 Taunton signs. Cross the swing bridge after 1¼ miles and bear left into Winterstoke Road; From East: Take M4 then M32 and follow signs for the City Centre. Then as for North and West; From South: Exit M5 at Junction 18 and follow Taunton signs over the swing bridge (then as above).
Bus Services: Services 27A and 28A from the Railway Station.

BRISTOL ROVERS FC

Founded: 1883 **(Entered League**: 1920)
Former Names: Black Arabs FC (1883-84); Eastville Rovers FC (1884-96); Bristol Eastville Rovers FC (1896-97)
Nickname: 'Pirates' 'Rovers'
Ground: Memorial Stadium, Filton Avenue, Bristol BS7 0AQ
Office: The Beeches, Broomhill Road, Brislington, Bristol BS4 5RG

Record Attendance: 9,173
Colours: Shirts – Blue & White Quarters Shorts – White
Telephone N°: (0117) 977-2000
Ticket Office: (0117) 924-3200
Fax Number: (0117) 977-3888
Pitch Size: 115 × 76 yards
Ground Capacity: Approximately 9,275
Seating Capacity: 1,871

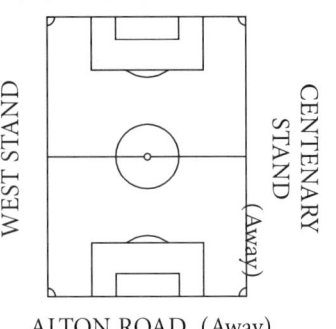

FILTON AVENUE
CLUB HOUSE TERRACE

WEST STAND

CENTENARY STAND (Away)

ALTON ROAD (Away)

GENERAL INFORMATION

Supporters Club: c/o 199 Two Mile Hill Road, Kingswood BS15 1AZ
Telephone N°: (0117) 961-1772
Car Parking: Approximately 300 spaces at ground (pre-booked) and street parking
Coach Parking: At the ground
Nearest Railway Station: Temple Meads (2 miles)
Nearest Bus Station: Bristol City Centre
Club Shop: 199 Two Mile Hill Road, Kingswood and Pirate Leisure, 411-413 Gloucester Road, Horfield, Bristol BS7 8TS
Opening Times: Supporters' Club: Weekdays 9.00am to 5.00pm and Saturdays 9.00am to 1.00pm. Pirate Leisure: Weekdays 10.00am to 5.00pm, Saturdays 9.00am to 1.00pm
Telephone N°: (0117) 961-1772 + (0117) 924-7474
Postal Sales: Yes
Nearest Police Station: Bridewell (2 miles)
Police Telephone N°: (0117) 927-7777

GROUND INFORMATION

Away Supporters' Entrances & Sections: Alton Road

ADMISSION INFO (1998/99 PRICES)

Adult Standing: £10.00
Adult Seating: £14.00 – £17.00
Child Standing: £4.50
Child Seating: £10.00 – £17.00
Programme Price: £2.00

DISABLED INFORMATION

Wheelchairs: Unspecified number accommodated in front of the Centenary Stand and West Stand
Helpers: One helper admitted per disabled person
Prices: Free of charge for the disabled and helpers
Disabled Toilets: Centenary Stand & West Stand
Are Bookings Necessary: Yes
Contact: (0117) 977-2000 (Club Secretary)

Travelling Supporters' Information:
Routes: From All Parts: Exit M32 at Junction 2 then take 3rd exit at the roundabout (signposted Horfield) into Muller Road. Continue for approximately 1½ miles passing straight across 3 sets of traffic lights. At the 6th set of traffic lights turn left into Filton Avenue and the ground is immediately on the left.

BURNLEY FC

Founded: 1882 (**Entered League**: 1888)	**Colours**: Shirts – Claret & Blue
Former Names: Burnley Rovers FC	Shorts – Claret
Nickname: 'Clarets'	**Telephone Nº**: (01282) 700000
Ground: Turf Moor, Brunshaw Road,	**Ticket Office**: (01282) 700010
Burnley, Lancashire BB10 4BX	**Fax Number**: (01282) 700014
Record Attendance: 54,775 (23/2/24)	**Pitch Size**: 114 × 72 yards
	Ground Capacity: 22,000 (All seats)

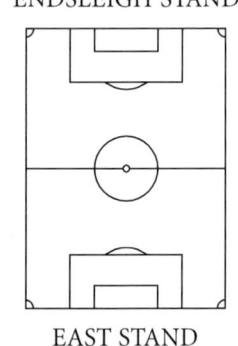

BELVEDERE ROAD
ENDSLEIGH STAND
BRUNSHAW ROAD
BOB LORD STAND
JAMES HARGREAVES STAND
EAST STAND

GENERAL INFORMATION

Supporters Club: David Spencer, c/o Club
Telephone Nº: (01282) 435176
Car Parking: Ormerod Road, adjacent to the Fire Station (2 minutes walk) and Fulledge Recreation Ground (2 minutes walk)
Coach Parking: By Police direction
Nearest Railway Stat'n: Burnley Central (1½ miles)
Nearest Bus Station: Burnley (5 minutes walk)
Club Shop: At Ground
Opening Times: 9.00am – 5.30pm Mondays to Thursdays; Fridays 9.00am – 7.00pm; Saturdays 9.00am – 5.30pm
Telephone Nº: (01282) 700016
Postal Sales: Yes
Nearest Police Station: Parker Lane, Burnley (5 minutes walk)
Police Telephone Nº: (01282) 425001

GROUND INFORMATION

Away Supporters' Entrances & Sections:
Endsleigh Stand

ADMISSION INFO (1998/99 PRICES)

Adult Seating: £9.00 – £14.00
Child Seating: £4.50 – £7.00
Programme Price: £1.70

DISABLED INFORMATION

Wheelchairs: Three designated wheelchair areas
Helpers: One helper admitted per disabled fan
Prices: Free for disabled. Concessionary for helpers
Disabled Toilets: Yes
Commentaries are available via headsets
Are Bookings Necessary: Yes
Contact: (01282) 700010 (Ticket Office)

Travelling Supporters' Information:

Routes: From North: Follow A682 to Town Centre and take first exit at roundabout (Gala Club) into Yorkshire Street. Follow through traffic signals into Brunshaw Road; From East: Follow A646 to A671 then along Todmorden Road towards Town Centre. At traffic signals (crossroads) turn right into Brunshaw Road; From West & South: Exit M6 at Junction 29 to M65. Exit M65 at Junction 10 and follow signs for Town Centre. At roundabout in centre take the third exit into Yorkshire Street. Then as North.

BURY FC

<table>
<tr><td>

Founded: 1885 (**Entered League**: 1894)
Former Names: None
Nickname: 'Shakers'
Ground: Gigg Lane, Bury, Lancashire
BL9 9HR
Record Attendance: 35,000 (9/1/60)
Pitch Size: 112 × 72 yards

</td><td>

Colours: Shirts – White
       Shorts – Royal Blue
Telephone Nº: (0161) 764-4881
Ticket Office: (0161) 764-4881
Fax Number: (0161) 764-5521/763-3103
Ground Capacity: 11,840
Seating Capacity: 9,340

</td></tr>
</table>

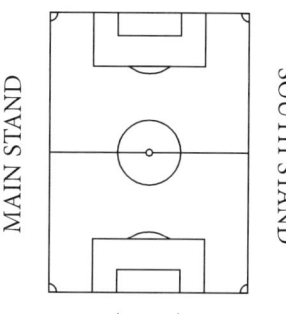

CEMETERY END STAND

MAIN STAND

SOUTH STAND

(Away)
MANCHESTER ROAD
STAND

GENERAL INFORMATION

Supporters Club: P. Cullen, c/o Club
Telephone Nº: –
Car Parking: Street Parking
Coach Parking: By Police direction
Nearest Railway Station: Bury Interchange (1 mile)
Nearest Bus Station: Bury Interchange
Club Shop: At Ground
Opening Times: Daily 9.00am to 5.00pm
Telephone Nº: (0161) 705-2144
Postal Sales: Yes (Price lists available)
Nearest Police Station: Irwell Street, Bury
Police Telephone Nº: (0161) 872-5050

GROUND INFORMATION

Away Supporters' Entrances & Sections:
Gigg Lane entrance for the Manchester Road Stand
(May be subject to change)

ADMISSION INFO (1998/99 PRICES)

Adult Standing: £12.00
Adult Seating: £12.00 – £16.00
Child Standing: £12.00
Child Seating: £7.00
Note: Family concessions are also available
Programme Price: £1.80

DISABLED INFORMATION

Wheelchairs: Spaces for 20 wheelchairs in disabled section (home area) and a further 6 spaces in the Away Supporters' Section
Helpers: One helper admitted per wheelchair
Prices: Free of charge for both disabled and helpers
Disabled Toilets: Available in disabled section
A Radio Commentary is available in the Press Box
Are Bookings Necessary: Yes
Contact: (0161) 764-4881

Travelling Supporters' Information:
Routes: From North: Exit M66 at Junction 2, take Bury Road (A58) for ½ mile, then turn left into Heywood Street and follow this into Parkhills Road until its end, turn left into Manchester Road (A56) and then left again into Gigg Lane. From South, East & West: Exit M60 at Junction 17, take Bury Road (A56) for 3 miles and then turn right into Gigg Lane.

CAMBRIDGE UNITED FC

Founded: 1919 (**Entered League:** 1970)
Former Names: Abbey Utd FC (1919-49)
Nickname: 'U's' 'United'
Ground: Abbey Stadium, Newmarket Road, Cambridge CB5 8LN
Record Attendance: 14,000 (1/5/70)
Pitch Size: 110 × 74 yards

Colours: Shirts – Amber
Shorts – Black
Telephone Nº: (01223) 566500
Ticket Office: (01223) 566500
Fax Number: (01223) 566502
Ground Capacity: 9,667
Seating Capacity: 3,265

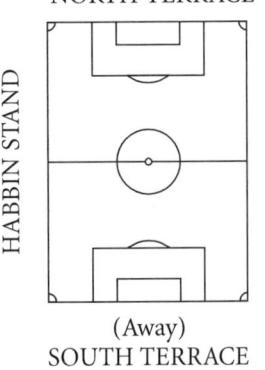

NEWMARKET ROAD
NORTH TERRACE

HABBIN STAND

Disabled

MAIN STAND

(Away)
SOUTH TERRACE

GENERAL INFORMATION
Supporters Club: c/o Club
Telephone Nº: (01223) 241771
Car Parking: Coldhams Common (No street parking)
Coach Parking: Coldhams Common
Nearest Railway Station: Cambridge (2 miles)
Nearest Bus Station: Cambridge City Centre
Club Shop: At Ground
Opening Times: Weekdays & Matchdays 10.00am to 5.00pm
Telephone Nº: (01223) 566503
Postal Sales: Yes
Nearest Police Station: Parkside, Cambridge
Police Telephone Nº: (01223) 358966

GROUND INFORMATION
Away Supporters' Entrances & Sections:
Coldham Common turnstiles 20-23 – South Terrace

ADMISSION INFO (1998/99 PRICES)
Adult Standing: £8.00
Adult Seating: £8.00 – £12.00
Child Standing: £5.00
Child Seating: £5.00 – £6.00
Programme Price: £1.50

DISABLED INFORMATION
Wheelchairs: 12 spaces in total for Home and Away fans in the disabled section, in front of Main Stand. Also 13 spaces available in North Terrace.
Helpers: One helper admitted per disabled fan
Prices: Free for the disabled. £8.00 for helpers
Disabled Toilets: Available at the rear of the disabled enclosure in the Main Stand
Are Bookings Necessary: Yes
Contact: (01223) 566500

Travelling Supporters' Information:
Routes: From North: Take A1 and A14 to Cambridge and then head towards Newmarket. Turn off onto the B1047, signposted for Cambridge Airport, Horningsea and Fen Ditton. Turn right at the top of the slip road and travel through Fen Ditton. Turn right at the traffic lights at the end of the village. Go straight on at the roundabout onto Newmarket Road. The ground is 500 yards on the left; From South & East: Take A10 or A130 into Cambridge and join A14. Then as North; From West: Take A 422 to Cambridge and join the A14. Then as North.
Bus Services: Services from Railway Station to City Centre and Nº 3 from City Centre to the Ground.

CARDIFF CITY FC

Founded: 1899 (**Entered League**: 1920) **Former Names**: Riverside FC (1899-1910) **Nickname**: 'Bluebirds' **Ground**: Ninian Park, Sloper Road, Cardiff CF1 8SX **Record Attendance**: 61,566 (14/10/61) **Pitch Size**: 110 × 70 yards	**Colours**: Shirts – Blue Shorts – White **Telephone Nº**: (01222) 398636 **Ticket Office**: (01222) 398636 **Fax Number**: (01222) 341148 **Ground Capacity**: 14,601 **Seating Capacity**: 11,371

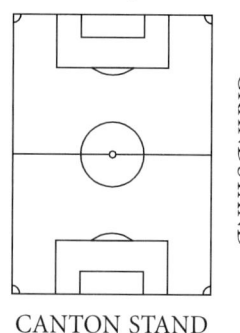

GRANGETOWN END
(Away)

POPULAR BANK

SLOPER ROAD GRANDSTAND

CANTON STAND

GENERAL INFORMATION

Supporters Club: Clive Francis, c/o Club
Telephone Nº:
Car Parking: Sloper Road & Street Parking
Coach Parking: Sloper Road (adjacent)
Nearest Railway Station: Cardiff Central (1 mile)
Nearest Bus Station: Cardiff Central
Club Shop: At Ground
Opening Times: Weekdays 9.00am – 5.00pm and
Matchdays 1½ hours before kick-off
Telephone Nº: (01222) 666699
Postal Sales: Yes
Nearest Police Station: Cowbridge Road East,
Cardiff (1 mile)
Police Telephone Nº: (01222) 222111

GROUND INFORMATION

Away Supporters' Entrances & Sections:
Grangetown End, Sloper Road entrances and
accommodation

ADMISSION INFO (1998/99 PRICES)

Adult Standing: £8.00
Adult Seating: £10.00 – £12.00
Child Standing: £4.00
Child Seating: £5.00 – £6.00
Programme Price: £1.60

DISABLED INFORMATION

Wheelchairs: 20 spaces available in total for Home
and Away fans in the disabled section, in the Canton
End Family Enclosure
Helpers: One helper admitted per disabled fan
Prices: Disabled and helpers free of charge
Disabled Toilets: Yes
Are Bookings Necessary: Yes, for away fans
Contact: (01222) 398636

Travelling Supporters' Information:
Routes: From All Parts: Exit M4 at Junction 33 and follow Penarth (A4232) signs. After 6 miles, take the B4267
to Ninian Park.

CARLISLE UNITED FC

Founded: 1903 (**Entered League**: 1928)
Former Names: Amalgamation of
Shadd-ongate United FC & Carlisle Red
Rose FC
Nickname: 'Cumbrians' 'Blues'
Ground: Brunton Park Stadium,
Warwick Road, Carlisle   CA1 1LL
Record Attendance: 27,500 (5/1/57)

Colours: Shirts – Royal Blue
               Shorts – White
Telephone Nº: (01228) 526237
Ticket Office: (01228) 526237
Fax Number: (01228) 530138
Pitch Size: 112 × 74 yards
Ground Capacity: 16,300
Seating Capacity: 7,129

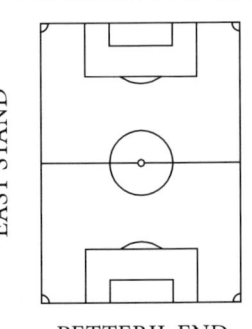

WARWICK ROAD END

EAST STAND

MAIN STAND
PADDOCK

PETTERIL END

GENERAL INFORMATION

Supporters Club: D. Tweddle, c/o Club
Telephone Nº: (01228) 524014
Car Parking: Rear of Ground via St. Aidans Road
Coach Parking: St. Aidans Road Car Park
Nearest Railway Station: Carlisle Citadel (1 mile)
Nearest Bus Station: Lowther Street, Carlisle
Club Shop: At Ground
Opening Times: Weekdays 9.00am – 5.00pm
Saturdays 10.00am – 4.00pm; Saturday Matchdays
9am–3pm + 4.45pm–5.30pm; Midweek Matchdays
9.00am–7.45pm and 9.30pm to 10.15pm
Telephone Nº: (01228) 524014
Postal Sales: Yes
Nearest Police Station: Rickergate, Carlisle (1½ mls)
Police Telephone Nº: (01228) 528191

GROUND INFORMATION

Away Supporters' Entrances & Sections:
Turnstiles 17-21 for the East Stand

ADMISSION INFO (1998/99 PRICES)

Adult Standing: £8.00
Adult Seating: £10.00 or £11.00
Child Standing: £5.00
Child Seating: £6.00 (in Family Stand)
Programme Price: £1.50

DISABLED INFORMATION

Wheelchairs: 17 spaces for wheelchairs in the
disabled section, in front of the New East Stand
Helpers: One helper admitted per disabled fan
Prices: Will advise when booking
Disabled Toilets: Yes
Are Bookings Necessary: Yes
Contact: (01228) 526237

Travelling Supporters' Information:
Routes: From North, South & East: Exit M6 at Junction 43 and follow signs for Carlisle (A69) into Warwick
Road; From West: Take A69 straight into Warwick Road.

CHARLTON ATHLETIC FC

Founded: 1905 (**Entered League:** 1921)
Former Names: None
Nickname: 'Addicks'
Ground: The Valley, Floyd Road,
Charlton, London SE7 8BL
Record Attendance: 75,031 (12/2/38)
Pitch Size: 111 × 73 yards

Colours: Shirts – Red
Shorts – White
Telephone Nº: (0181) 333-4000
Ticket Office: (0181) 333-4010
Fax Number: (0181) 333-4021
Ground Capacity: 20,000 (All seats)

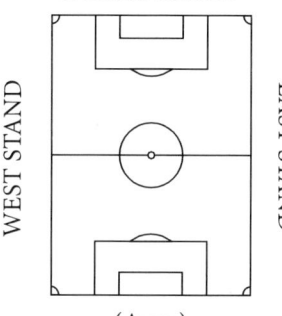

HARVEY GARDENS
NORTH STAND

WEST STAND

EAST STAND

(Away)
THE JIMMY SEED STAND
VALLEY GROVE

GENERAL INFORMATION

Supporters Club: P.O. Box 387, London   SE9 6EH
Telephone Nº: (0181) 265-5283
Car Parking: Street Parking
Coach Parking: By Police direction
Nearest Railway Station: Charlton (2 minutes walk)
Nearest Bus Station: –
Club Shop: At Ground
Opening Times: Weekdays 10.00am – 6.00pm
Saturdays 8.30am – 12.00pm
Telephone Nº: (0181) 333-4035
Postal Sales: Yes
Nearest Police Station: Greenwich (2 miles)
Police Telephone Nº: (0181) 853-8212

GROUND INFORMATION

Away Supporters' Entrances & Sections:
Valley Grove/Jimmy Seed Stand

ADMISSION INFO (1997/98 PRICES)

Adult Seating: £8.00 or £13.00 Members
£13.00 or £15.00 Non-members
Child Seating: £4.00 – £9.00
(Junior Reds £1.00 in Family Area)
Note: 1998/99 Matchday admission prices were not
fixed at the time of going to press
Programme Price: £1.80

DISABLED INFORMATION

Wheelchairs: 40 spaces in total for Home and Away
fans in the disabled areas, West Stand and East Stand
Helpers: Up to 40 helpers admitted
Prices: Free of charge for disabled fans and helpers
Disabled Toilets: Available in West and East Stands
Commentaries are available – please ring for details
Are Bookings Necessary: Yes
Contact: (0181) 333-4010

Travelling Supporters' Information:
Routes: From All Parts: Exit M25 at Junction 2 (A2 London-bound) and follow until the road becomes A102(M).
Take the exit marked Woolwich Ferry and turn right along the A206 Woolwich Road. Turn right at the first set of
traffic lights and Floyd Road is the 2nd turning on the left.

CHELSEA FC

Founded: 1905 **(Entered League:** 1905)
Former Names: None
Nickname: 'Blues'
Ground: Stamford Bridge, Fulham
Road, London   SW6 1HS
Record Attendance: 82,905 (12/10/35)
Pitch Size: 113 × 74 yards

Colours: Shirts – Blue
                    Shorts – Blue
Telephone Nº: (0171) 385-5545
Ticket Office: (0171) 386-7799
Fax Number: (0171) 381-4831
Ground Capacity: 35,250 (All seats)
Note: Redevelopment is progressing

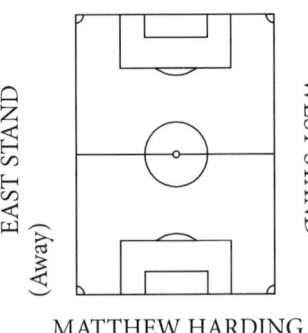

UMBRO SHED END

EAST STAND (Away)

WEST STAND

MATTHEW HARDING
STAND

GENERAL INFORMATION

Membership Office: Joanne Griffith, c/o Club
Telephone Nº: (0171) 385-5545
Car Parking: Underground car park at ground
Coach Parking: By Police direction
Nearest Tube Station: Fulham Broadway (District)
Club Shop: Chelsea Megastore – at the ground
Opening Times: Weekdays 10.00am – 6.00pm and
Matchdays
Telephone Nº: (0171) 565-1490
Chelsea Megastore Fax: (0171) 565-1491
Postal Sales: Yes – Mail Order (0870) 603-0005
Nearest Police Station: Fulham
Police Telephone Nº: (0171) 385-1212

GROUND INFORMATION

Away Supporters' Entrances & Sections:
East Stand entrances and accommodation

ADMISSION INFO (1998/99 PRICES)

Adult Seating: £22.00 – £28.00
Child Seating: £10.00 (Members only in the
Members Section)
Programme Price: £2.50

DISABLED INFORMATION

Wheelchairs: 40 spaces in total for Home and Away
fans in the disabled area
Helpers: One helper admitted per disabled person
Prices: Prices on application
Disabled Toilets: Available in the East Stand
Concourse and also in the Matthew Harding Stand
Are Bookings Necessary: Yes
Contact: (0171) 385-5545

Travelling Supporters' Information:
Routes: From North & East: Follow Central London signs from A1/M1 to Hyde Park Corner, then signs for
Guildford (A3) to Knightsbridge (A4). After 1 mile turn left into Fulham Road; From South: Take A13 or A24
then A219 to cross Putney Bridge and follow signs for 'West End' (A304) to join the A308 into Fulham Road; From
West: Take M4 then A4 to Central London, then signs to Westminster (A3220). After ∫ mile, turn right at the
crossroads into Fulham Road.

CHESTER CITY FC

Founded: 1884 (**Entered League:** 1931)	**Colours:** Shirts – Blue and White Stripes
Former Names: Chester FC	Shorts – Blue and White
Nickname: 'Blues' 'City'	**Telephone Nº:** (01244) 371376
Ground: The Deva Stadium, Bumpers	**Ticket Office:** (01244) 371376
Lane, Chester CH1 4LT	**Fax Number:** (01244) 390265
Record Attendance: 5,638 (2/4/94)	**Ground Capacity:** 6,000
Pitch Size: 115 × 75 yards	**Seating Capacity:** 3,408

SOUTH TERRACE
(Away)

EAST STAND
Jewson Family Area

WEST STAND

NORTH TERRACE

GENERAL INFORMATION
Supporters Club: B. Hipkiss, c/o Club
Telephone Nº: (01244) 371376
Car Parking: Ample at ground
Coach Parking: At ground
Nearest Railway Station: Chester (1½ miles)
Nearest Bus Station: Chester (¾ mile)
Club Shop: At Ground
Opening Times: Weekdays & matchdays 9am – 5pm
Telephone Nº: (01244) 390243
Postal Sales: Yes
Nearest Police Station: Chester (¾ mile)
Police Telephone Nº: (01244) 350222

GROUND INFORMATION
Away Supporters' Entrances & Sections:
South Terrace for covered accommodation

ADMISSION INFO (1998/99 PRICES)
Adult Standing: £7.50
Adult Seating: £10.00   (concessions available
Child Standing: £4.00   in the Family Enclosure)
Child Seating: £5.00
Programme Price: £1.50

DISABLED INFORMATION
Wheelchairs: 72 spaces in total for Home and Away fans in the disabled areas, West Stand and East Stand
Helpers: One helper admitted per disabled person
Prices: Free for the disabled. Helpers normal price
Disabled Toilets: Available in West and East Stands
Are Bookings Necessary: Yes
Contact: (01244) 371376

Travelling Supporters' Information:
Routes: From North: Take the M56, A41 or A56 into the Town Centre and then follow Queensferry (A548) signs into Sealand Road. Turn left at the traffic lights by 'Texas' into Bumpers Lane – the ground is ½ mile at the end of the road; From East: Take A54 or A51 into the Town Centre (then as North); From South: Take A41 or A483 into Town Centre (then as North); From West: Take A55, A494 or A548 and follow Queensferry signs towards Birkenhead (A494) and after 1¼ miles bear left onto the A548 (then as North); From M6/M56 (Avoiding Town Centre): Take M56 to Junction 16 (signposted Queensferry), turn left at the roundabout onto A5117, signposted Wales. At next roundabout turn left onto the A5480 (signposted Chester) and after approximately 3 miles take the 3rd exit from the roundabout (signposted Sealand Road Industrial Parks). Go straight across 2 sets of traffic lights into Bumpers Lane. The ground is ½ mile on the right.

CHESTERFIELD FC

Founded: 1866 **(Entered League**: 1899)	**Colours**: Shirts – Blue and White
Former Names: Chesterfield Town FC	Shorts – White
Nickname: 'Spireites' 'Blues'	**Telephone Nº**: (01246) 209765
Ground: Recreation Ground, Saltergate,	**Ticket Office**: (01246) 209765
Chesterfield S40 4SX	**Fax Number**: (01246) 556799
Record Attendance: 30,968 (7/4/39)	**Ground Capacity**: 8,954
Pitch Size: 112 × 73 yards	**Seating Capacity**: 2,608

SALTERGATE
SPION KOP

MAIN STAND
ST. MARGARET'S DRIVE

COMPTON STREET SIDE

(Away)
CROSS STREET END

GENERAL INFORMATION

Supporters Club: c/o Club
Telephone Nº: (01246) 231535
Car Parking: Saltergate Car Parks (½ mile)
Coach Parking: By Police direction
Nearest Railway Station: Chesterfield (1 mile)
Nearest Bus Station: Chesterfield
Club Shop: At Ground
Opening Times: Weekdays and Matchdays 9.00am
to 5.00pm
Telephone Nº: (01246) 231535
Postal Sales: Yes
Nearest Police Station: Chesterfield (¾ mile)
Police Telephone Nº: (01246) 220100

GROUND INFORMATION

Away Supporters' Entrances & Sections:
Cross Street turnstiles for Cross Street End (open)

ADMISSION INFO (1998/99 PRICES)

Adult Standing: £8.50
Adult Seating: £9.50 – £10.50
Child Standing: £4.00
Child Seating: £5.00
Home Fans Only – Family Stand Tickets:
1 Adult + 1 Child – £11.50
Programme Price: £1.60

DISABLED INFORMATION

Wheelchairs: 20 spaces in total for Home and Away
fans below the Saltergate Wing Stand
Helpers: One helper admitted per disabled person
Prices: Free of charge for disabled. Helpers £9.50
Disabled Toilets: One available underneath the
Main Stand
Are Bookings Necessary: Yes
Contact: (01246) 209765

Travelling Supporters' Information:
Routes: From North: Exit M1 at Junction 30 then take the A619 into the Town Centre. Follow signs for Old
Brampton into Saltergate; From South and East: Take A617 into Town Centre (then as North); From West: Take
A619 and when into the Town take the 1st exit at the roundabout into Foljambe Road. Follow to the end of the
road, then turn right into Saltergate.

COLCHESTER UNITED FC

Founded: 1937 (**Entered League**: 1950)	**Colours**: Shirts – Royal blue & white stripes
Former Names: The Eagles	Shorts – White
Nickname: 'U's'	**Telephone Nº**: (01206) 508800
Ground: Layer Road Ground,	**Ticket Office**: (01206) 508800
Colchester CO2 7JJ	**Fax Number**: (01206) 508803
Record Attendance: 19,072 (27/11/48)	**Ground Capacity**: 7,555
Pitch Size: 110 × 70 yards	**Seating Capacity**: 1,965

LAYER ROAD END
(Away)

POPULAR SIDE

FAMILY ENCLOSURE

MAIN STAND

NEW CLOCK END

GENERAL INFORMATION

Supporters Club: Chris Hazlehurst, c/o Club
Telephone Nº: (01206) 508800
Car Parking: Street Parking
Coach Parking: Boadicea Way (¼ mile)
Nearest Railway Station: Colchester North (2 miles)
Nearest Bus Station: Colchester Town Centre
Club Shop: At ground + 2nd shop in Town Centre
Opening Times: At ground: Thursdays and
Matchdays 10.30am – 3.30pm
Town Centre: Monday to Saturday 9.00am – 5.30pm
Telephone Nº: (01206) 508800
Postal Sales: Yes
Nearest Police Stat'n: Southway, Colchester (½ml.)
Police Telephone Nº: (01206) 762212

GROUND INFORMATION

Away Supporters' Entrances & Sections:
Layer Road End turnstiles

ADMISSION INFO (1998/99 PRICES)

Adult Standing: £7.00
Adult Seating: £7.00   £9.00
Child Standing: £3.50 – £4.50
Child Seating: £3.50 – £4.50
Note: Further concessions are available in the
Family Area
Programme Price: £1.50

DISABLED INFORMATION

Wheelchairs: 12 spaces in total for Home and Away
fans on the Terrace next to the Main Stand
Helpers: One helper admitted per wheelchair
Prices: Free for disabled. Terrace price for helpers
Disabled Toilets: Available under the Main Stand
Commentaries are available for up to 3 people
Are Bookings Necessary: Yes
Contact: (01206) 508800

Travelling Supporters' Information:
Routes: From North: Take A134, B1508 or A12 into the Town Centre then follow signs to Layer (B1026) into Layer Road; From South: Take A12 and follow signs to Layer (B1026) into Layer Road; From West: Take A604 or A120 into the Town Centre then follow signs to Layer (B1026) into Layer Road.

COVENTRY CITY FC

Founded: 1883 (**Entered League:** 1919)
Former Names: Singers FC (1883-1898)
Nickname: 'Sky Blues'
Ground: Highfield Road Stadium, King Richard Street, Coventry CV2 4FW
Record Attendance: 51,455 (29/4/67)
Pitch Size: 110 × 76 yards

Colours: Shirts – Sky Blue / White Trim
Shorts – Sky Blue
Telephone Nº: (01203) 234000
Ticket Office: (01203) 234020
Fax Numbers: (01203) 234099 (General Office); (01203) 234023 (Ticket Office)
Ground Capacity: 23,627 (All seats)

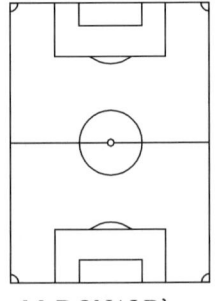

SWAN LANE
COMTEL EAST STAND
(THACKHALL STREET) MITCHELLS & BUTLER STAND
KING RICHARD STREET MAIN STAND
McDONALD's FAMILY STAND
CO-OP BANK
WEST TERRACE

GENERAL INFORMATION
Supporters Club: 'The Members Club', Highfield Road Stadium, Coventry CV2 4FW
Telephone Nº: (01203) 234004 **Fax:** (01203) 234015
Car Parking: Street Parking
Coach Parking: By Police direction
Nearest Railway Station: Coventry (1 mile)
Nearest Bus Station: Coventry (1 mile)
Bus Services to Ground: C16/C35/C36/C37/C7/C8/C24/C26/C27/C31A/C31C/C32/66/778
Club Shop: At Ground
Opening Times: Daily except Sundays (office hours)
Telephone Nº: (01203) 234030
Postal Sales: Yes
Nearest Police Station: Little Park Street (1 mile)
Police Telephone Nº: (01203) 539010

GROUND INFORMATION
Away Supporters' Entrances & Sections:
Thackhall Street for Mitchells & Butler Stand

ADMISSION INFO (1998/99 PRICES)
Adult Seating: £17.00 – £23.00
Child Seating: £8.50 – £11.50
Programme Price: £2.00

DISABLED INFORMATION
Wheelchairs: 70 spaces in total for Home and Away fans in the disabled section in the Clock Stand
Helpers: Up to 68 helpers admitted
Prices: Free for the disabled. Helpers £18.00
Disabled Toilets: 2 are adjacent to the disabled area
Commentaries available via Hospital Radio
Are Bookings Necessary: Yes
Contact: (01203) 234020

Travelling Supporters' Information:
Routes: From North & South: Exit M6 at Junction 2, take A4600 and follow signs for City Centre. Cross the roundabout keeping along Ansty Road (A4600). The road bears left, take the right exit at the next roundabout and continue for ¼ mile. Turn right into Swan Lane and the ground is directly ahead; From the East: Exit M69 at Junction with M6 then as above; From the West: Exit M40 at Junction 15 and follow A46 for approx. 10 miles until first traffic island. Go straight on until second island and turn left onto B4110 signposted 'Stoke'. At the next roundabout take the third exit and turn first left. Turn left into Walsgrave Road and first right into Swan Lane.

CREWE ALEXANDRA FC

Founded: 1877 (**Entered League**: 1892)	**Colours**: Shirts – Red
Former Names: None	Shorts – White
Nickname: 'Railwaymen'	**Telephone Nº**: (01270) 213014
Ground: Gresty Road Ground, Crewe,	**Ticket Office**: (01270) 252610
Cheshire CW2 6EB	**Fax Number**: (01270) 216320
Record Attendance: 20,000 (30/1/60)	**Ground Capacity**: 5,900
Pitch Size: 112 × 74 yards	**Seating Capacity**: 4,536

FAMILY STAND

RINGWAY STAND

MAIN STAND

(Away)
GRESTY ROAD END

GENERAL INFORMATION

Supporters Club: c/o Glynn Steele, 18 Gresty Road, Crewe
Telephone Nº: (01270) 213014 ext. 108
Car Parking: Car Park at ground (400 cars)
Coach Parking: Car Park at ground
Nearest Railway Station: Crewe (5 minutes walk)
Nearest Bus Station: Crewe Town
Club Shop: At Ground
Opening Times: Monday to Friday and Matchdays 9.00am – 5.00pm
Telephone Nº: (01270) 213014
Postal Sales: Yes
Nearest Police Station: Crewe Town (1 mile)
Police Telephone Nº: (01270) 500222

GROUND INFORMATION

Away Supporters' Entrances & Sections:
Gresty Road Entrances for Gresty Road seating

ADMISSION INFO (1998/99 PRICES)

Adult Standing: £11.50
Adult Seating: £13.50
OAP Standing: £8.50
OAP Seating: £10.50
Child Standing: £6.00
Child Seating: £6.00
Programme Price: £2.00

DISABLED INFORMATION

Wheelchairs: Approximately 17 spaces in total in the disabled areas, Family Stand, Ringway Stand + 10 at the Away end
Helpers: One helper admitted per disabled person
Prices: £5.00 in total for each disabled fan & helper
Disabled Toilets: Available in the Family Stand, Ringway Stand and the Visitors End
Commentaries are available for the blind
Are Bookings Necessary: Yes
Contact: (01270) 213014

Travelling Supporters' Information:
Routes: From North: Exit M6 at Junction 17 and take Crewe (A534) road, and at Crewe roundabout follow Chester signs into Nantwich Road. The take a left turn into Gresty Road; From South & East: Take A52 to A5020, then on to Crewe roundabout (then as North); From West: Take A534 into Crewe and turn right just before the railway station into Gresty Road.

CRYSTAL PALACE FC

Founded: 1905 (**Entered League**: 1920)
Former Names: None
Nickname: 'Eagles'
Ground: Selhurst Park, London
SE25 6PU
Record Attendance: 51,482 (11/5/79)
Pitch Size: 110 × 74 yards

Colours: Shirts – Red with Blue Trim
Shorts – Red
Telephone Nº: (0181) 768-6000
Ticket Office: (0181) 771-8841
Fax Number: (0181) 768-6003
Ground Capacity: 26,309 (All seats)

HOLMESDALE ROAD
STAND

PARK ROAD
ARTHUR WAIT STAND

CLIFTON ROAD
MAIN STAND

WHITEHORSE
LANE STAND

GENERAL INFORMATION
Supporters Club: Daniel Griffin, c/o Club
Telephone Nº: (0181) 768-6000
Car Parking: Street Parking & Sainsbury Car Park
near the ground
Coach Parking: Thornton Heath
Nearest Railway Station: Selhurst/Norwood
Junction (5 minutes walk)
Nearest Bus Station: Norwood Junction
Club Shop: At Ground
Opening Times: Weekdays & Matchdays 9.30–5.30
Telephone Nº: (0181) 768-6100
Postal Sales: Yes
Nearest Police Station: South Norwood (15 mins.
walk)
Police Telephone Nº: (0181) 653-8568

GROUND INFORMATION
Away Supporters' Entrances & Sections:
Park Road for the Arthur Wait Stand

ADMISSION INFO (1998/99 PRICES)
Adult Seating: £16.00 to £20.00
Child Seating: £12.00 to £15.00
Note: Prices vary depending on the game
Programme Price: £2.00

DISABLED INFORMATION
Wheelchairs: 24 spaces for Home fans; 4 spaces for
Away fans in disabled area, Holmesdale Road Stand
& also 12 spaces in Arthur Wait Stand
Helpers: One helper admitted per wheelchair
Prices: Free for the disabled. Helpers pay full price
Disabled Toilets: Located in the disabled section
Commentaries are available for 12 people
Are Bookings Necessary: Yes
Contact: (0181) 768-6000

Travelling Supporters' Information:
Routes: From North: Take M1/A1 to North Circular (A406) to Chiswick. Then take the South Circular (A205) to Wandsworth and then the A3 to the A214 and follow signs to Streatham to the A23. Turn left onto the B273 after 1 mile, follow to the end and turn left into the High Street and into Whitehorse Lane; From East: Take A232 (Croydon Road) to Shirley and join A215 (Northwood Road). After 2¼ miles turn left into Whitehorse Lane; From South: Take A23 and follow signs for Crystal Palace (B266) through Thornton Heath into Whitehorse Lane; From West: Take the M4 to Chiswich (then as North).

DARLINGTON FC

Founded: 1883 **(Entered League**: 1921)	**Colours**: Shirts – White and Black
Former Names: None	Shorts – Black
Nickname: 'Quakers'	**Telephone Nº**: (01325) 465097
Ground: Feethams Ground, Darlington,	**Ticket Office**: (01325) 465097
DL1 5JB	**Fax Number**: (01325) 381377
Record Attendance: 21,023 (14/11/60)	**Ground Capacity**: 7,750
Pitch Size: 110 × 74 yards	**Seating Capacity**: 4,750

VICTORIA ROAD
FEETHAMS CRICKET GROUND

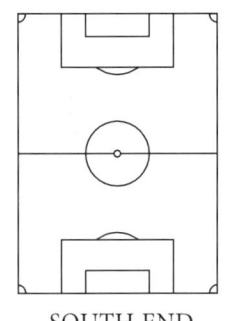

SOUTH END
POLAM LANE

GENERAL INFORMATION
Supporters Club: c/o K. Davies, 60 Harrison Terrace, Darlington
Telephone Nº: (01325) 350161
Car Parking: Street Parking
Coach Parking: By Police direction
Nearest Railway Station: Darlington
Nearest Bus Station: Darlington Central
Club Shop: At Ground
Opening Times: Monday – Friday 9.00am – 5.00pm
Telephone Nº: (01325) 465097
Postal Sales: Yes
Nearest Police Station: Park Police Station, Darlington (¼ mile)
Police Telephone Nº: (01325) 467681

GROUND INFORMATION
Away Supporters' Entrances & Sections:
Polam Lane turnstiles for South Terrace (open) and the West Stand

ADMISSION INFO (1998/99 PRICES)
Adult Standing: £8.00
Adult Seating: £11.00
Child Standing: £5.00
Child Seating: £6.00
Programme Price: £1.50

DISABLED INFORMATION
Wheelchairs: 30 spaces in total for Home and Away fans in the disabled section, East Stand
Helpers: One helper admitted per disabled person
Prices: Free of charge for Disabled and Helpers
Disabled Toilets: Yes
Are Bookings Necessary: Yes
Contact: (01325) 465097

Travelling Supporters' Information:
Routes: From North: Take A1(M) to A167 and follow road to the Town Centre, then follow Northallerton signs to Victoria Road; From East: Take A67 to the Town Centre (then as North); From South: Take A1(M) then A66(M) into the Town Centre and then take the 3rd exit at the second roundabout into Victoria Road; From West: Take A67 into the Town Centre and then take the 3rd exit at the roundabout into Victoria Road.

DERBY COUNTY FC

Founded: 1884 (**Entered League**: 1888)	**Colours**: Shirts – White with Black trim
Former Names: None	Shorts – Black with White trim
Nickname: 'Rams'	**Telephone Nº**: (01332) 202202
Ground: Pride Park Stadium, Royal Way,	**Ticket Office**: (01332) 209209
Pride Park, Derby DE24 8XL	**Fax Number**: (01332) 667519
Record Attendance: –	**Ground Capacity**: 30,800 (All seats)
Pitch Size: 115 × 75 yards	

NORTH STAND

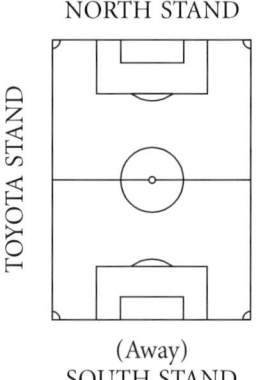

TOYOTA STAND

EAST STAND

(Away)
SOUTH STAND

GENERAL INFORMATION

Supporters Club: Mr E. Hallam, c/o Club
Telephone Nº: (01332) 202202
Car Parking: Spaces for 1,200 cars at the ground
Coach Parking: At the ground
Nearest Railway Station: Derby Midland (1 mile)
Nearest Bus Station: Derby Central
Club Shop: Rams Super Store
Opening Times: Weekdays 9.00am – 6.00pm and Matchdays. Sundays 10.00am to 4.00pm
Telephone Nº: (01332) 209000
Postal Sales: Yes
Nearest Police Station: Cotton Lane, Derby
Police Telephone Nº: (01332) 290100

GROUND INFORMATION

Away Supporters' Entrances & Sections:
South Stand

ADMISSION INFO (1998/99 PRICES)

Adult Seating: £14.00 – £26.00
Child Seating: £7.00 – £13.00
Note: Prices vary according to the category of game
Programme Price: £2.00

DISABLED INFORMATION

Wheelchairs: 204 spaces available in total
Helpers: One helper admitted for each disabled fan
Prices: £14.00 for the each disabled fan & helper
Disabled Toilets: Yes
Are Bookings Necessary: Yes
Contact: (01332) 202202

Travelling Supporters' Information:
Routes: From All Parts: Exit the M1 at Junction 25 and follow A52 towards the City Centre until the ground is signposted on the left. Follow the signs for the ground.
From Train Station: The Stadium is 10 minutes walk by way of a tunnel under the railway opposite Brunswick Inn, Station Approach. Then follow the footpath; Buses: Shuttle service from the bus station from 1.00pm until 2.45pm on Saturdays. Similar service 6.00 – 7.30pm midweek games. Return shuttles available post-match.

EVERTON FC

Founded: 1878 (**Entered League**: 1888)	**Colours**: Shirts – Blue
Former Names: St. Domingo's FC (1878-1879)	Shorts – White
Nickname: 'Blues' 'Toffeemen'	**Telephone Nº**: (0151) 330-2200
Ground: Goodison Park, Goodison Road, Liverpool L4 4EL	**Ticket Office**: (0151) 330-2300
Record Attendance: 78,299 (18/9/48)	**Fax Number**: (0151) 523-9666
	Pitch Size: 112 × 78 yards
	Ground Capacity: 40,000 (All seats)

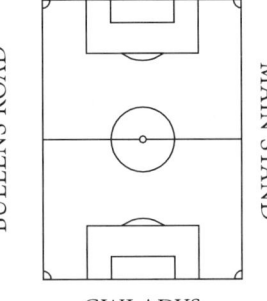

GOODISON AVENUE
PARK END

BULLENS ROAD

GOODISON ROAD
MAIN STAND

GWLADYS
STREET END

GENERAL INFORMATION

Supporters Club: The Secretary, c/o Club
Telephone Nº: (0151) 330-2208
Car Parking: Corner of Priory Road and Utting Ave.
Coach Parking: Priory Road
Nearest Railway Station: Liverpool Lime Street
Nearest Bus Station: Moss Street, Liverpool
Club Shop: 'Megastore' At Ground
Opening Times: Weekdays and Matchdays 9.00am to 5.00pm and Evening Matches
Telephone Nº: (0151) 330-2333
Postal Sales: Yes – Mail Order and Credit Card Sales
Nearest Police Station: Walton Lane, Liverpool
Police Telephone Nº: (0151) 709-6010

GROUND INFORMATION

Away Supporters' Entrances & Sections:
Bullens Road entrances for Bullens Stand

ADMISSION INFO (1998/99 PRICES)

Adult Seating: £14.00 – £19.00
Child Seating: £8.00 – £19.00
Note: There are no concessionary prices available in certain areas of the ground
Programme Price: £2.00

DISABLED INFORMATION

Wheelchairs: 48 spaces for home fans, 13 spaces for away fans in the disabled section, Bullens Road
Helpers: One helper admitted per wheelchair
Prices: Free for the disabled. Helpers £14.00
Disabled Toilets: Available in the disabled section
Commentaries are available for the blind
Are Bookings Necessary: Yes
Contact: (0151) 330-2300

Travelling Supporters' Information:
Routes: From North: Exit M6 at Junction 24. Take A58 Liverpool Road to A580 and follow into Walton Hall Avenue; From South and East: Exit M6 at Junction 21A onto the M62. At the end of the M62 turn right into Queen's Drive. After 3¾ miles turn left into Walton Hall Avenue; From North Wales: Cross the Mersey into the City Centre and follow signs to Preston (A580) into Walton Hall Avenue.
Bus Services: Services from the City Centre – 19, 20, 21, F1, F9, F2, 30

EXETER CITY FC

Founded: 1904 (**Entered League**: 1920)	**Colours**: Shirts – Red and White Stripes
Former Names: Amalgamation of	Shorts – White
St. Sidwell United FC & Exeter United FC	**Telephone N°**: (01392) 254073
Nickname: 'Grecians'	**Ticket Office**: (01392) 254073
Ground: St. James Park, Exeter EX4 6PX	**Fax Number**: (01392) 425885
Record Attendance: 20,984 (4/3/31)	**Ground Capacity**: 10,570
Pitch Size: 114 × 73 yards	**Seating Capacity**: 1,690

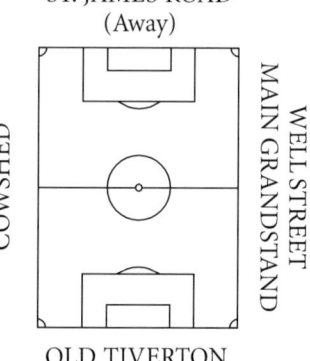

ST. JAMES ROAD
(Away)

COWSHED

MAIN GRANDSTAND

WELL STREET

OLD TIVERTON
ROAD END

GENERAL INFORMATION

Supporters Club: c/o Club
Telephone N°: (01392) 254073
Car Parking: King William Street
Coach Parking: Paris Street Bus Station
Nearest Railway Station: Exeter St. James Park (adjacent)
Nearest Bus Station: Paris Street Bus Station
Club Shop: At Ground
Opening Times: Weekdays and Matchdays 9.00am to 5.00pm
Telephone N°: (01392) 254073
Postal Sales: Yes
Nearest Police Station: Heavitree Road (½ mile)
Police Telephone N°: (01392) 252101

GROUND INFORMATION

Away Supporters' Entrances & Sections:
St. James Road turnstiles for St. James Rd. Enclosure

ADMISSION INFO (1998/99 PRICES)

Adult Standing: £8.00
Adult Seating: £10.00
Child Standing: £5.00   (Home Under 16's – £2.00)
Programme Price: £1.70

DISABLED INFORMATION

Wheelchairs: Limited number of spaces available in front of the Grandstand
Helpers: One helper admitted per wheelchair
Prices: Free of charge for both disabled and helpers
Disabled Toilets: None
Are Bookings Necessary: Yes
Contact: (01392) 254073

Travelling Supporters' Information:
Routes: From North: Exit M5 at Junction 30 and follow signs to the City Centre along Sidmouth Road and onto Heavitree Road. Take the 4th exit at the roundabout into Western Way and 2nd exit into Tiverton Road then next left into St. James Road; From East: Take A30 into Heavitree Road (then as North); From South & West: Take A38 and follow City Centre signs into Western Way and take the third exit at the roundabout into St. James Road.
Note: This ground is very difficult to find being in a residential area on the side of a hill without prominent floodlights.

FULHAM FC

Founded: 1879 (**Entered League**: 1907)
Former Names: Fulham St. Andrew's FC
(1879-1898)
Nickname: 'Cottagers'
Ground: Craven Cottage, Stevenage
Road, Fulham, London SW6 6HH
Record Attendance: 49,335 (8/10/38)

Colours: Shirts – White
Shorts – Black
Telephone Nº: (0171) 384-4720
Ticket Office: (0171) 384-4710
Fax Number: (0171) 384-4715
Pitch Size: 117 × 75 yards
Ground Capacity: 18,900
Seating Capacity: 6,900

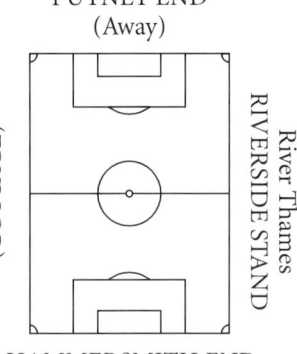

PUTNEY END
(Away)

STEVENAGE ROAD STAND (COTTAGE)

RIVERSIDE STAND

River Thames

HAMMERSMITH END

GENERAL INFORMATION

Supporters Club: Ms. A. Monks, c/o The Club
Telephone Nº: (0171) 736-6561
Car Parking: Street Parking and Henry Compton
School, Kingswood Road
Coach Parking: Stevenage Road
Nearest Railway Station: Putney
Nearest Tube Station: Putney Bridge (District)
Club Shop: At the ground and Fulham Road
Opening Times: At the ground: Matchdays only,
Saturdays 11.00am to 6.00pm, Tuesdays 5.30pm to
10.30pm; Fulham Road: Monday to Saturday
10.00am to 6.00pm
Telephone Nº: (0171) 736-3292 (Ground) ??
Postal Sales: Yes
Nearest Police Station: Heckfield Place, Fulham
Police Telephone Nº: (0171) 385-1212

GROUND INFORMATION

Away Supporters' Entrances & Sections:
Putney End for the Putney Terrace (open)

ADMISSION INFO (1998/99 PRICES)

Adult Standing: £10.00
Adult Seating: £14.00
Child Standing: £5.00
Child Seating: £7.00
Programme Price: £2.00

DISABLED INFORMATION

Wheelchairs: 15 spaces for Home and Away fans, in
the North-West corner of the Stadium
Helpers: One helper admitted per disabled person
Prices: Free for the disabled. Helpers £10.00
Disabled Toilets: By forecourt – opposite Cottage
Are Bookings Necessary: Yes
Contact: (0171) 736-6561

Travelling Supporters' Information:
Routes: From North: Take A1/M1 to North Circular (A406) west to Neasden and follow signs for Harlesdon A404, then Hammersmith A219. At Broadway, follow Fulham sign and turn right after 1 mile into Harboard Street then left at the end for the ground; From South & East: Take South Circular (A205), follow Putney Bridge sign (A219). Cross bridge and follow Hammersmith signs for ½mile, turn left into Bishops Park Road, then right at the end; From West: Take M4 to A4. Branch left after 2 miles into Hammersmith Broadway (then as North).

GILLINGHAM FC

Founded: 1893 **(Entered League:** 1920)
Former Names: New Brompton FC
(1893-1913)
Nickname: 'Gills'
Ground: Priestfield Stadium, Redfern
Avenue, Gillingham, Kent ME7 4DD
Pitch Size: 114 × 75 yards
Record Attendance: 23,002 (10/1/48)

Colours: Shirts – Blue
   Shorts – Blue
Telephone Nº: (01634) 851854
Ticket Office: (01634) 851462
Fax Number: (01634) 850986
Ground Capacity: Approximately 9,000
Seating Capacity: 3,590

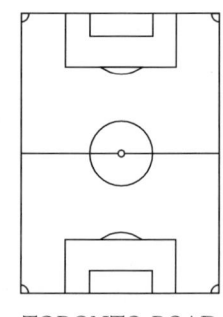

PRIESTFIELD ROAD
GILLINGHAM END

GORDON ROAD STAND (NEW STAND)

REDFERN AVENUE MAINSTAND

TORONTO ROAD
RAINHAM END

GENERAL INFORMATION

Supporters Club: Peter Lloyd, c/o The Club
Telephone Nº: (01634) 851854
Car Parking: Street Parking
Coach Parking: By Police direction
Nearest Railway Station: Gillingham
Nearest Bus Station: Gillingham
Club Shop: At the Gillingham and Rainham Ends
of the ground
Opening Times: Weekdays and Matchdays 10.00am
to 5.00pm
Telephone Nº: (01634) 851462
Postal Sales: Yes
Nearest Police Station: Gillingham
Police Telephone Nº: (01634) 234488

GROUND INFORMATION

Away Supporters' Entrances & Sections:
Redfern Avenue turnstiles for Redfern Avenue
Corner (Gillingham End)

ADMISSION INFO (1998/99 PRICES)
Adult Standing: £9.50
Adult Seating: £11.00 – £16.00
Child Standing: £4.50
Child Seating: £6.00 – £16.00
Note: Concessions only available in certain sections
Programme Price: £1.80

DISABLED INFORMATION
Wheelchairs: 16 spaces in total for Home and Away
fans in the disabled section, in the New Stand
Helpers: One helper admitted per disabled person
Prices: Free for the disabled. Helpers normal prices
Disabled Toilets: Available in the New Stand
Are Bookings Necessary: Preferred
Contact: (01634) 851462

Travelling Supporters' Information:
Routes: From All Parts: Exit M2 at Junction 4 and follow the link road (dual carriageway) B278 to the 3rd
roundabout. Turn left onto the A2 (dual carriageway) and go across the roundabout to the traffic lights. Turn
right into Woodlands Road after the traffic lights. The ground is ˇ mile on the left.

GRIMSBY TOWN FC

Founded: 1878 **(Entered League:** 1892)
Former Names: Grimsby Pelham FC
(1879)
Nickname: 'Mariners'
Ground: Blundell Park, Cleethorpes,
DN35 7PY
Record Attendance: 31,651 (20/2/37)

Colours: Shirts – Black and White Stripes
Shorts – Black
Telephone Nᵒ: (01472) 697111
Ticket Office: (01472) 697111
Fax Number: (01472) 693665
Pitch Size: 111 × 74 yards
Ground Capacity: 8,870 (All seats)

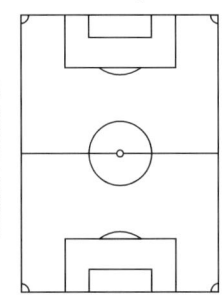

NEVILLE STREET
OSMOND STAND
(Away)

HARRINGTON STREET
MAIN STAND

GRIMSBY ROAD
JOHN SMITH'S STAND

PONTOON STAND
BLUNDELL AVENUE

GENERAL INFORMATION
Supporters Club: c/o Rachel Branson,
26 Humberstone Road, Grimsby
Telephone Nᵒ: (01472) 360050
Car Parking: Street Parking
Coach Parking: Harrington Street – Near ground
Nearest Railway Station: Cleethorpes (1½ miles)
Nearest Bus Station: Brighowgate, Grimsby (4 mls)
Club Shop: At Ground
Opening Times: Monday – Friday 9.00am – 5.00pm
Match Saturdays 10.00am to kick-off
Telephone Nᵒ: (01472) 697111
Postal Sales: Yes
Nearest Police Station: Cleethorpes (1½ miles)
Police Telephone Nᵒ: (01472) 359171

GROUND INFORMATION
Away Supporters' Entrances & Sections:
Harrington Street turnstiles 15-18

ADMISSION INFO (1998/99 PRICES)
Adult Seating: £11.00 – £14.00 (Away fans £13.00)
Senior Citizens: £7.00
Child Seating: £5.00
Note: Special Family rate in the Main Stand
Programme Price: £1.50

DISABLED INFORMATION
Wheelchairs: 50 spaces in total for Home and Away
fans in the disabled section, Main Stand
Helpers: Helpers are admitted
Prices: Free for disabled. Helpers normal prices
Disabled Toilets: Available in disabled section
Commentaries are available in disabled section
Are Bookings Necessary: No
Contact: (01472) 697111

Travelling Supporters' Information:
Routes: From All Parts except Lincolnshire and East Anglia: Take M180 to A180 and follow signs for Grimsby/
Cleethorpes. The A180 ends at a roundabout (the 3rd in short distance after crossing docks), take 2nd exit from
the roundabout over the Railway flyover into Cleethorpes Road (A1098) and continue into Grimsby Road. After
second stretch of dual carriageway, the ground is ½ mile on the left; From Lincolnshire: Take A46 or A16 and
follow Cleethorpes signs along (A1098) Weelsby Road for 2 miles. Take the 1st exit at the roundabout at the end of
Clee Road into Grimsby Road. The ground is 1¾ miles on the right.

HALIFAX TOWN FC

Founded: 1911 (**Entered League:** 1921)	**Colours:** Shirts – Blue
Former Names: None	Shorts – Black
Nickname: 'Shaymen'	**Telephone Nº:** (01422) 345543
Ground: Shay Ground, Shay Syke,	**Ticket Office:** (01422) 345543
Halifax HX1 2YS	**Fax Number:** (01422) 349487
Record Attendance: 36,885 (14/2/53)	**Ground Capacity:** 7,800
Pitch Size: 110 × 75 yards	**Seating Capacity:** 1,896

SOUTH STAND
OPEN TERRACE

MAIN STAND

Huddersfield Road (A629)
SKIRCOAT STAND

NORTH STAND
HUNGER HILL

GENERAL INFORMATION

Supporters Club: Stephen Kell, c/o Halifax Promotions, Shay Ground, Halifax
Telephone Nº: (01422) 353423
Car Parking: Shaw Hill Car Park (Nearby)
Coach Parking: Shaw Hill
Nearest Railway Station: Halifax (3 minutes walk)
Nearest Bus Station: Halifax (10 minutes walk)
Club Shop: Westgate, Halifax
Opening Times: Weekdays (except Fridays) 10.00am to 5.00pm. Matchdays 10.00am to 2.30pm
Telephone Nº: (01422) 353423
Postal Sales: Yes
Nearest Police Station: Halifax (1¼ miles)
Police Telephone Nº: (01422) 360333

GROUND INFORMATION

Away Supporters' Entrances & Sections:
North Stand, Hunger Hill accommodation

ADMISSION INFO (1998/99 PRICES)

Adult Standing: £8.00
Adult Seating: £9.00
Child Standing: £4.00   (Under 12's £2.00)
Child Seating: £5.00   (Under 12's £3.00)
Programme Price: £2.00

DISABLED INFORMATION

Wheelchairs: 10 spaces in total in the disabled section, Edgar Street side, 12 spaces on the new North Terrace
Helpers: Helpers admitted at usual prices
Prices: Normal prices
Disabled Toilets: In the Main Stand and the new North Terrace
Are Bookings Necessary: No
Contact: (01422) 345543

Travelling Supporters' Information:
Routes: From the North: Take the A629 to Halifax Town Centre. Take the 2nd exit at the roundabout into Broad Street and follow signs for Huddersfield (A629) into Skircoat Road; From the South, East and West: Exit the M62 at Junction 24 and follow Halifax (A629) signs to Town Centre into Skircoat Road then Shaw Hill for ground.

HARTLEPOOL UNITED FC

Founded: 1908 (**Entered League**: 1921)
Former Names: Hartlepools United FC
(1908-68); Hartlepool FC (1968-77)
Nickname: 'The Pool'
Ground: Victoria Park, Clarence Road,
Hartlepool   TS24 8BZ
Record Attendance: 17,426 (15/1/57)

Colours: Shirts – Royal Blue and White
              Shorts – Royal Blue
Telephone Nº: (01429) 272584
Ticket Office: (01429) 272584
Fax Number: (01429) 863007
Pitch Size: 113 × 77 yards
Ground Capacity: 7,229
Seating Capacity: 3,966

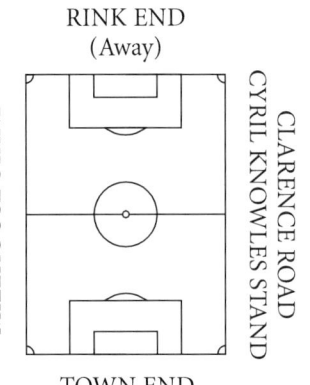

RINK END
(Away)

RABY ROAD
MILLHOUSE STAND

CLARENCE ROAD
CYRIL KNOWLES STAND

TOWN END

GENERAL INFORMATION
Supporters Club: c/o D. Latimer, 4 Friarage
Gardens, Hartlepool
Telephone Nº: (01429) 261197
Car Parking: Street Parking
Coach Parking: Church Street
Nearest Railway Station: Hartlepool Church Street
(5 minutes walk)
Club Shop: At Ground
Opening Times: Weekdays 10.00am – 2.00pm and
Saturdays 10.00am – 2.00pm. Closed Wednesdays
Telephone Nº: (01429) 272584
Postal Sales: Yes
Nearest Police Station: Avenue Road, Hartlepool
Police Telephone Nº: (01429) 221151

GROUND INFORMATION
Away Supporters' Entrances & Sections:
Clarence Road turnstiles 1 & 2 for Rink End

ADMISSION INFO (1998/99 PRICES)
Adult Standing: £9.00
Adult Seating: £11.00
Child Standing: £7.00
Child Seating: £8.00
Programme Price: £1.50

DISABLED INFORMATION
Wheelchairs: 20 spaces in total for Home and Away
fans in the disabled section, Cyril Knowles Stand
Helpers: One helper admitted per wheelchair
Prices: £6.00 each for the Disabled and Helpers
Disabled Toilets: Available in Cyril Knowles Stand
Are Bookings Necessary: Advisable for large
numbers
Contact: (01429) 272584

Travelling Supporters' Information:
Routes: From North: Take A1/A19 then A179 towards Hartlepool to Hart. Straight across traffic lights (2½
miles) to the cross-roads, then turn left into Clarence Road; From South and West: Take A1/A19 or A689 into
Town Centre then turn left into Middleton Road and left again into Clarence Road.

HUDDERSFIELD TOWN FC

Founded: 1908 (**Entered League:** 1910)
Former Names: None
Nickname: 'Terriers'
Ground: The Alfred McAlpine Stadium, Huddersfield   HD1 6PX
Record Attendance: 18,820 (26/12/97)
Pitch Size: 115 × 76 yards

Colours: Shirts – Blue and White Stripes
Shorts – White
Telephone Nº: (01484) 484100
Ticket Office: (01484) 484123
Fax Number: (01484) 484101
Ground Capacity: 24,000 (All seats)

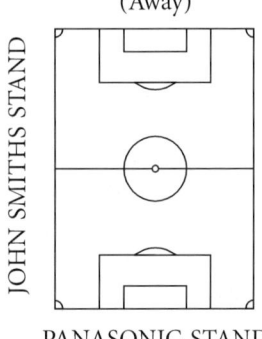

GARDNER MERCHANT STAND (Away)

JOHN SMITHS STAND

LAWRENCE BATLEY STAND

PANASONIC STAND

GENERAL INFORMATION

Supporters Club: Mrs P.A. Richardson, 3 Bradley Quarry Close, Bradley, Huddersfield   HD2 1XQ
Telephone Nº: (01484) 315620
Car Parking: Car park for 1,100 cars adjacent (pre-sold)
Coach Parking: Adjacent car park
Nearest Railway Station: Huddersfield (1¼ miles)
Nearest Bus Station: Huddersfield
Club Shop: At Ground
Opening Times: Weekdays 9.00am – 5.00pm and Saturday Matchdays 9.00am – 3.00pm
Telephone Nº: (01484) 484144
Postal Sales: Yes
Nearest Police Station: Huddersfield (1 mile)
Police Telephone Nº: (01484) 422122

GROUND INFORMATION

Away Supporters' Entrances & Sections:
Gardner Merchant Stand

ADMISSION INFO (1998/99 PRICES)

Adult Seating: £12.00 to £15.00
Child Seating: £6.00 to £8.00
Programme Price: £1.80

DISABLED INFORMATION

Wheelchairs: 169 spaces in total for home and away fans in the disabled sections, Riverside Stand, Gardner Merchant Stand and John Smiths Stand
Helpers: One helper admitted per wheelchair
Prices: Concessionary rates for disabled and helpers
Disabled Toilets: Available in the disabled sections Commentaries are available for the blind
Are Bookings Necessary: Yes – for certain games
Contact: (01484) 484100

Travelling Supporters' Information:
Routes: From North, East and West: Exit M62 at Junction 25 and take the A644 and A62 following Huddersfield signs. Follow signs for the Alfred McAlpine Stadium; From South: Leave M1 at Junction 38 and follow A637/A642 to Huddersfield. At the Ring Road, follow signs for the A62 to Alfred McAlpine Stadium.

HULL CITY FC

Founded: 1904 (**Entered League**: 1905)	**Colours**: Shirts – Black and Amber
Former Names: None	Shorts – Black
Nickname: 'Tigers'	**Telephone Nº**: (01482) 327200
Ground: Boothferry Park, Boothferry	**Ticket Office**: (01482) 506666
Road, Hull HU4 6EU	**Fax Number**: (01482) 565752
Record Attendance: 55,019 (26/2/49)	**Ground Capacity**: 11,500
Pitch Size: 115 × 75 yards	**Seating Capacity**: 5,495

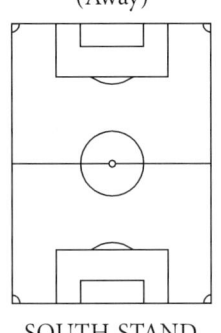

BOOTHFERRY ROAD
NORTH TERRACE
(Away)

NORTH ROAD MAIN STAND

EAST STAND

SOUTH STAND

GENERAL INFORMATION

Supporters Club: F. Anholm, c/o The Club
Telephone Nº: –
Car Parking: Limited parking at the ground, street parking and schools
Coach Parking: At the ground
Nearest Railway Station: Hull Paragon (1½ miles)
Nearest Bus Station: Ferensway, Hull (1½ miles)
Club Shop: At the ground
Opening Times: Matchdays only 10.00am to 4.30pm
Telephone Nº: (01482) 351119/328297
Postal Sales: Yes
Nearest Police Station: Central, Hull (2 miles)
Police Telephone Nº: (01482) 210031

GROUND INFORMATION

Away Supporters' Entrances & Sections:
North Stand turnstiles for North Terrace

ADMISSION INFO (1998/99 PRICES)

Adult Standing: £8.00
Adult Seating: £9.00 – £11.00
Child Standing: £4.00
Child Seating: £5.00 – £6.00
Programme Price: £1.50

DISABLED INFORMATION

Wheelchairs: 20 spaces in total for Home and Away fans in the disabled section, South East Corner
Helpers: One helper admitted per disabled person
Prices: Free of charge for disabled. Helpers £8.00
Disabled Toilets: One available within disabled area
Commentaries are available for the blind
Are Bookings Necessary: No
Contact: (01482) 327200

Travelling Supporters' Information:

Routes: From North: Take A1 or A19 then A1079 into the City Centre and follow signs for Leeds (A63) into Anlaby Road. After 1 mile take the 1st exit at the roundabout into Boothferry Road; From West: Take M62 to A63 to Hull. Fork left after Ferriby Crest Motel to the Humber Bridge roundabout, then take the 1st exit to Boothferry Road – the ground is 1½ miles. Do NOT follow Clive Sullivan Way; From South: Non-scenic alternative route take M18 to M62 (then as West). Or use motorways M1 to M18, then M180 and follow signs over Humber Bridge (Toll), take 2nd exit at roundabout (A63) towards Boothferry Road (the ground is 1½miles).

IPSWICH TOWN FC

Founded: 1878 (**Entered League**: 1938)
Former Names: None
Nickname: 'Town'; 'Super Blues'
Ground: Portman Road, Ipswich
IP1 2DA
Record Attendance: 38,010 (8/3/75)
Pitch Size: 112 × 70 yards

Colours: Shirts – Blue with White Sleeves
Shorts – White
Telephone Nº: (01473) 400500
Ticket Office: (01473) 400555
Fax Number: (01473) 400040
Ground Capacity: 22,600 (All seats)

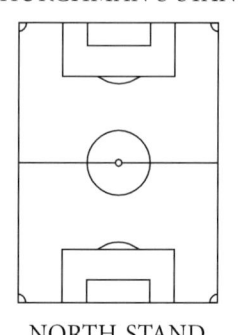

CHURCHMAN'S STAND

PORTMAN ROAD (Away) COBBOLD STAND

CONSTANTINE ROAD PIONEER STAND

NORTH STAND
PORTMAN WALK

GENERAL INFORMATION
Supporters Club: Mr G. Dodson, c/o The Club
Telephone Nº: (01473) 400500
Car Parking: Portman Road and Portman Walk car parks
Coach Parking: Portman Walk
Nearest Railway Station: Ipswich (5 minutes walk)
Nearest Bus Station: Ipswich
Club Shop: At Ground
Opening Times: Weekdays and Matchdays 9.00am to 5.00pm
Telephone Nº: (01473) 400501
Postal Sales: Yes
Nearest Police Station: Civic Drive, Ipswich (5 minutes walk)
Police Telephone Nº: (01473) 233000

GROUND INFORMATION
Away Supporters' Entrances & Sections:
Portman Road turnstiles

ADMISSION INFO (1998/99 PRICES)
Adult Seating: £13.00 – £25.00
Child Seating: £3.00 – £6.00
Pensioners Seating: £9.00 – £11.00
Programme Price: £1.50

DISABLED INFORMATION
Wheelchairs: 30 spaces + 50 seats for home fans, 6 spaces + 14 seats for away fans – in Pioneer Stand
Helpers: One helper admitted per disabled person
Prices: Free of charge for disabled. Helpers £13.00
Disabled Toilets: Adjacent to the disabled area
Commentaries are available for the blind
Are Bookings Necessary: Yes
Contact: (01473) 219211

Travelling Supporters' Information:
Routes: From North and West: Take A1214 from A14/A12 following signs for Ipswich West only. Proceed through Post House Hotel traffic lights and at the 2nd set of traffic lights turn right into West End Road. The ground is ¼ mile along on the left; From South: Follow signs for Ipswich West, then as North and West (above).

LEEDS UNITED FC

Founded: 1919 (**Entered League:** 1920)
Former Names: Formed after Leeds City
FC were wound up for 'Irregular Practices'
Nickname: 'United'
Ground: Elland Road, Leeds   LS11 0ES
Record Attendance: 57,892 (15/3/67)
Pitch Size: 114 × 70 yards

Colours: Shirts – White
  Shorts – White
Telephone Nº: (0113) 226-6000
Ticket Office: (0113) 226-1000
Fax Number: (0113) 226-6050
Ground Capacity: 40,204 (All seats)

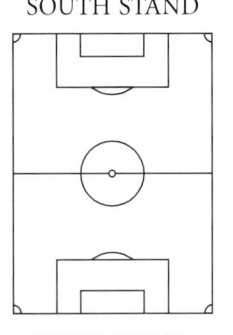

ELLAND ROAD
SOUTH STAND

LOWFIELDS ROAD
EAST STAND

WEST STAND

REVIE STAND

GENERAL INFORMATION

Supporters Club: Eric Carlile, c/o The Club
Telephone Nº: (0113) 226-6000
Car Parking: Large car parks (adjacent)
Coach Parking: By Police direction
Nearest Railway Station: Leeds City (1½ miles)
Nearest Bus Station: Leeds City Centre – specials
from Swinegate
Club Shop: At Ground
Opening Times: Weekdays 9.15am – 5.00pm,
Matchdays 9.15am – kick-off
Telephone Nº: (0113) 225-1144
Postal Sales: Yes (send SAE)
Nearest Police Station: Holbeck, Leeds (3 miles)
Police Telephone Nº: (0113) 243-5353

GROUND INFORMATION

Away Supporters' Entrances & Sections:
South East Corner or South Stand

ADMISSION INFO (1998/99 PRICES)

Adult Seating: £20.00 – £30.00
Child Seating: £12.00 – £20.00
Note: Prices vary according to the category of game
played.
Programme Price: £2.00

DISABLED INFORMATION

Wheelchairs: 103 spaces in total in the disabled
sections, West Stand and South West Corner
Helpers: One helper admitted per disabled person
Prices: Free of charge for the disabled. Helpers are
charged £16.00 – £19.00
Disabled Toilets: One adjacent to each of the
disabled sections
Commentaries via headphones in the West Stand
Are Bookings Necessary: Yes
Contact: (0113) 226-6000 (Ms. Sam Riley)

Travelling Supporters' Information:
Routes: From North: Take A58 or A61 into the City Centre and follow signs to M621. Leave the Motorway after
1½ miles and exit the roundabout onto A643 into Elland Road; From North-East: Take A63 or A64 into the City
Centre (then as North); From South: Take M1 to M621 (then as North); From West: Take M62 to M621 (then as
North).

LEICESTER CITY FC

Founded: 1884 (**Entered League**: 1894)	**Colours**: Shirts – Blue
Former Names: Leicester Fosse FC	Shorts – White
(1884-1919)	**Telephone N°**: (0116) 291-5000
Nickname: 'Filberts' 'Foxes'	**Ticket Office**: (0116) 291-5232
Ground: City Stadium, Filbert Street,	**Fax Number**: (0116) 247-0585
Leicester LE2 7FL	**Pitch Size**: 110 × 76 yards
Record Attendance: 47,298 (18/2/28)	**Ground Capacity**: 22,000 (All seats)

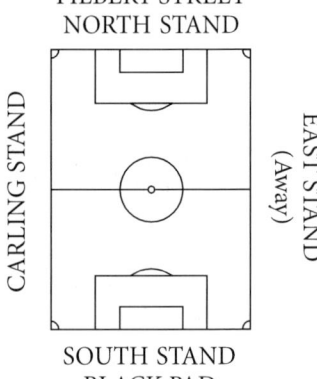

FILBERT STREET
NORTH STAND

CARLING STAND

BURNMOOR STREET
EAST STAND
(Away)

SOUTH STAND
BLACK PAD

GENERAL INFORMATION

Supporters Club: C. Ginetta, c/o The Club
Telephone N°: (0116) 291-5000
Car Parking: NCP Car Park (5 minutes walk)
Coach Parking: Sawday Street
Nearest Railway Station: Leicester (1 mile)
Nearest Bus Station: St. Margaret's (1 mile)
Club Shop: At Ground
Opening Times: Weekdays and Matchdays 9.00am
to 5.30pm
Telephone N°: (0116) 291-5253
Postal Sales: Yes
Nearest Police Station: Charles Street, Leicester
Police Telephone N°: (0116) 222-2222

GROUND INFORMATION

Away Supporters' Entrances & Sections:
East Stand, Blocks T and U

ADMISSION INFO (1998/99 PRICES)

Adult Seating: £15.00 – £24.50
Child Seating: £7.50 – £12.50
Programme Price: £2.00

DISABLED INFORMATION

Wheelchairs: 58 spaces for home fans, 17 spaces for
away fans in the disabled sections, Carling Stand,
South Stand Lower Tier and East Stand Block T
Helpers: One helper admitted per disabled person
Prices: Free of charge for disabled. Helpers £15.00
Disabled Toilets: Available in Carling Stand and
East Stand Block T
Are Bookings Necessary: Yes
Contact: (0116) 291-5296

Travelling Supporters' Information:
Routes: From the North: Take A46/A607 into the City Centre or exit M1 at Junction 21, take the A5460, turn
right ¾ mile after the Railway Bridge into Upperton Road, then right into Filbert Street; From the East: Take A47
into the City Centre (then as North); From the South: Exit M1 at Junction 21 and take A5460, turn right ¾ mile
after Railway Bridge into Upperton Road, then right into Filbert Street; From the West: Take M69 to the City Centre (then as North).

LEYTON ORIENT FC

Founded: 1881 (**Entered League:** 1905)
Former Names: Glyn Cricket & Football Club (1881/86); Eagle FC (1886/88); Clapton Orient FC (1888/1946); Leyton Orient FC (1946/66); Orient FC (1966/87)
Nickname: 'O's'
Record Attendance: 34,345 (21/1/64)

Colours: Shirts – Red;   Shorts – Black
Telephone Nº: (0181) 926-1111
Ticket Office: (0181) 926-1010
Fax Number: (0181) 926-1110
Pitch Size: 115 × 80 yards
Ground Capacity: 13,842
Seating Capacity: 7,169

Ground: Matchroom Stadium, Brisbane Road, Leyton, London   E10 5NE

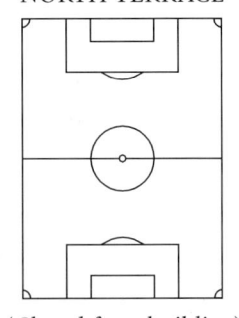

WINDSOR ROAD
NORTH TERRACE
OLIVER ROAD
WEST STAND
BRISBANE ROAD
MAIN STAND
(Closed for rebuilding)
BUCKINGHAM ROAD

GENERAL INFORMATION
Supporters Club: D. Dodd, c/o The Club
Telephone Nº: (0181) 539-6156
Car Parking: Street parking
Coach Parking: By Police direction
Nearest Railway Station: Leyton Midland Road (½ mile)
Nearest Tube Station: Leyton (Central)
Club Shop: At Ground
Opening Times: Weekdays 10.00am – 5.00pm
Telephone Nº: (0181) 539-1009
Postal Sales: Yes
Nearest Police Station: Francis Road, Leyton
Police Telephone Nº: (0181) 556-8855

GROUND INFORMATION
Away Supporters' Entrances & Sections:
South Wing turnstiles for South Wing Section

ADMISSION INFO (1998/99 PRICES)
Adult Standing: £10.00
Adult Seating: £11.00 – £13.00
Child Standing: £6.00
Child Seating: £7.00 – £9.00
Programme Price: £1.50

DISABLED INFORMATION
Wheelchairs: 18 spaces in total for Home and Away fans in the disabled section, North Terrace
Helpers: One helper admitted per disabled person
Prices: Free of charge for Disabled and Helpers
Disabled Toilets: Available near the disabled section
Commentaries are available – contact Football in the Community: (0181) 926-1015
Are Bookings Necessary: Yes
Contact: (0181) 556-5973

Travelling Supporters' Information:
Routes: From North & West: Take A406 North Circular, follow signs for Chelmsford to Edmonton. After 2½ miles take 3rd exit at roundabout towards Leyton (A112). Pass railway station and turn right after ½ mile into Windsor Road and left into Brisbane Road; From East: Follow A12 to London then City for Leytonstone. Follow Hackney signs into Grove Road, cross Main Road into Ruckholt Road then turn right into Leyton High Road, turn left after ¼ mile into Buckingham Road and left into Brisbane Road; From South: Take A102M through Blackwall Tunnel, follow signs for Newmarket (A102) to join A11 to Stratford, then follow signs for Stratford Station into Leyton Road to railway station (then as North).

LINCOLN CITY FC

Founded: 1884 (**Entered League:** 1892)	**Colours:** Shirts – Red with black & white
Former Names: None	Shorts – Black
Nickname: 'Red Imps'	**Telephone Nº:** (01522) 880011
Ground: Sincil Bank, Lincoln LN5 8LD	**Ticket Office:** (01522) 880011
Record Attendance: 23,196 (15/11/67)	**Fax Number:** (01522) 880020
Pitch Size: 110 × 76 yards	**Ground Capacity:** 11,721
	Seating Capacity: 8,283

STACEY WEST STAND
(Away)

SINCIL BANK
SIMONS STAND

ST. ANDREW'S STAND

THE ECHO

SOUTH PARK
STAND

GENERAL INFORMATION

Supporters Club: c/o The Club
Telephone Nº: (01522) 880011
Car Parking: Street parking
Coach Parking: South Common (300 yards)
Nearest Railway Station: Lincoln Central
Club Shop: At the ground
Opening Times: Weekdays & Matchdays 9.00am to 5.00pm
Telephone Nº: (01522) 880011
Postal Sales: Yes
Nearest Police Station: West Parade, Lincoln (1½ miles)
Police Telephone Nº: (01522) 529911

GROUND INFORMATION

Away Supporters' Entrances & Sections:
Stacey West standing accommodation. Turnstiles 4-8

ADMISSION INFO (1998/99 PRICES)

Adult Standing: £13.00
Adult Seating: £10.00 – £13.00
Child Standing: £8.00
Child Seating: £6.00 – £8.00
Programme Price: £1.70

DISABLED INFORMATION

Wheelchairs: Limited number of spaces available in the disabled section, adjacent to turnstile 23
Helpers: One helper admitted per disabled person
Prices: Applications for disabled passes must be made to the club. The disabled are admitted free of charge. Helpers pay usual prices
Disabled Toilets: Adjacent to disabled area
Are Bookings Necessary: Yes
Contact: (01522) 880011

Travelling Supporters' Information:
Routes: From East: Take A46 or A158 into the City Centre following Newark (A46) signs into High Street and take next left (Scorer Street and Cross Street) for the ground; From North & West: Take A15 or A57 into the City Centre, then as East; From South: Take A1 to A46 for the City Centre, then into High Street and turn right into Scorer Street, then right again into Cross Street for the ground.

LIVERPOOL FC

Founded: 1892 **(Entered League**: 1893)	**Colours**: Shirts – Red + White Markings
Former Names: None	Shorts – Red + White Markings
Nickname: 'Reds'	**Telephone Nº**: (0151) 263-2361
Ground: Anfield Road, Liverpool	**Ticket Office**: (0151) 260-8680;
L4 0TH	(0151) 263-5727 (Credit Card bookings)
Record Attendance: 61,905 (2/2/52)	**Fax Number**: (0151) 260-8813
Pitch Size: 110 × 74 yards	**Ground Capacity**: 45,100 (All seats)

WALTON BRECK ROAD
KOP STAND

CENTENARY STAND — PADDOCK ENCLOSURE — MAIN STAND — LOTHAIR ROAD

(Away)
ANFIELD ROAD STAND

GENERAL INFORMATION

Supporters Club: Liverpool International Supporters' Club, c/o Liverpool FC
Telephone Nº: (0151) 263-2361
Car Parking: Stanley Park car park (adjacent)
Coach Parking: Priory Road and Pinehurst Avenue
Nearest Railway Station: Kirkdale (¾ mile)
Nearest Bus Station: Paradise Street, Liverpool
Club Shop: At Ground
Opening Times: Monday to Friday 9.30am to 5.00pm and Saturdays 9.30am to 4.00pm
Telephone Nº: (0151) 263-1760
Postal Sales: Yes
Nearest Police Station: Walton Lane (1½ miles)
Police Telephone Nº: (0151) 709-6010

GROUND INFORMATION

Away Supporters' Entrances & Sections:
Anfield Road

ADMISSION INFO (1998/99 PRICES)

Adult Seating: £18.00
Kop Seating: £16.00
Programme Price: £2.00

DISABLED INFORMATION

Wheelchairs: 40 spaces for home fans only in the Paddock Enclosure and Kop Stand
Helpers: One helper admitted per wheelchair
Prices: £3.00 per disabled fan. £18 or £16 per helper
Disabled Toilets: One available in the Paddock, two in the Kop Stand
Commentaries are available for the blind
Are Bookings Necessary: Yes
Contact: (0151) 260-8680

Travelling Supporters' Information:
Routes: From North: Exit M6 at Junction 28 and follow Liverpool A58 signs into Walton Hall Avenue, pass Stanley Park and turn left into Anfield Road; From South and East: Take M62 to the end of the motorway, then turn right into Queen's Drive (A5058) and turn left after 3 miles into Utting Avenue. After 1 mile, turn right into Anfield Road; From North Wales: Take the Mersey Tunnel into the City Centre and follow signs for Preston (A580) into Walton Hall Avenue. Turn right into Anfield Road before Stanley Park.

LUTON TOWN FC

Founded: 1885 (**Entered League**: 1897)
Former Names: Formed by amalgamation
of Wanderers FC and Excelsior FC
Nickname: 'Hatters'
Ground: Kenilworth Road Stadium,
1 Maple Road, Luton   LU4 8AW
Record Attendance: 30,069 (4/3/59)

Colours: Shirts – white/royal blue/orange
Shorts – blue/orange/white trim
Telephone Nº: (01582) 411622
Ticket Office: (01582) 416976
Fax Number: (01582) 405070
Pitch Size: 110 × 72 yards
Ground Capacity: 9,970 (All seats)

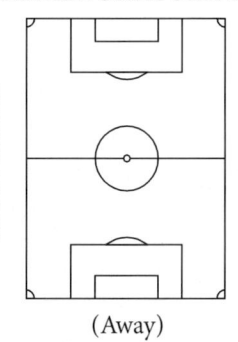

KENILWORTH ROAD
KENILWORTH STAND

MAPLE ROAD
MAIN STAND

BEECH HILL PATH
EXECUTIVE BOXES

(Away)
OAK STAND
OAK ROAD

GENERAL INFORMATION
Supporters Club: c/o Club Ticket Office
Telephone Nº: (01582) 416976
Car Parking: Street Parking
Coach Parking: Luton Bus Station
Nearest Railway Station: Luton (1 mile)
Nearest Bus Station: Bute Street, Luton
Club Shop: Kenilworth Road Forecourt
Opening Times: 10.00am – 4.00pm
Telephone Nº: (01582) 411622
Postal Sales: Yes
Nearest Police Stat'n: Buxton Road, Luton (¾ mile)
Police Telephone Nº: (01582) 401212

GROUND INFORMATION
Away Supporters' Entrances & Sections:
Oak Road for the Oak Stand

ADMISSION INFO (1998/99 PRICES)
Adult Seating: £8.50 – £17.00
Child Seating: £6.00 – £8.50
Programme Price: £1.80
Note: Lower prices apply when tickets are purchased
at least 14 days before the game and different prices
apply for certain cup games.

DISABLED INFORMATION
Wheelchairs: 15 spaces in total for Home and Away
fans in the disabled section in the Main Stand
Helpers: One helper admitted per disabled person
Prices: Free of charge for Disabled and Helpers
Disabled Toilets: Available adjacent to disabled area
Commentaries are available for the blind
Are Bookings Necessary: Yes
Contact: (01582) 411622

Travelling Supporters' Information:
Routes: From North and West: Exit M1 at Junction 11 and follow signs for Luton (A505) into Dunstable Road.
Follow the one-way system and turn right back towards Dunstable, take the first left into Oak Road; From South
and East: Exit M1 at Junction 10 (or A6/A612) into Luton Town Centre and follow signs into Dunstable Road.
After the railway bridge, take the sixth turning on the left into Oak Road.

MACCLESFIELD TOWN FC

Founded: 1874 (**Entered League**: 1997)	**Colours**: Shirts – Blue
Former Names: Macclesfield FC	Shorts – White
Nickname: 'The Silkmen'	**Telephone Nº**: (01625) 264686
Ground: Moss Rose Ground, London	**Ticket Office**: (01625) 264686
Road, Macclesfield, Cheshire SK11 7SP	**Fax Number**: (01625) 264692
Record Attendance: 10,041 (1948)	**Ground Capacity**: 6,578
Pitch Size: 110 × 72 yards	**Seating Capacity**: 2,753

STAR LANE TERRACE & STAND

LONDON ROAD TERRACE MAIN STAND

ESTATE ROAD STAND

(Away)
SILKMAN TERRACE

GENERAL INFORMATION

Supporters Club: Carole Wood, 178 Warwick Road, Macclesfield
Telephone Nº: (01625) 617670
Car Parking: Ample available near the ground
Coach Parking: Near the ground
Nearest Railway Station: Macclesfield (1 mile)
Nearest Bus Station: Macclesfield
Club Shop: At ground
Opening Times: Weekdays and matchdays 9.00am to 5.00pm
Telephone Nº: (01625) 264686
Postal Sales: Yes
Nearest Police Station: Macclesfield
Police Telephone Nº: (01625) 610000

GROUND INFORMATION

Away Supporters' Entrances & Sections:
Silkman Terrace

ADMISSION INFO (1998/99 PRICES)

Adult Standing: £10.00
Adult Seating: £12.00 and £14.00
Child Standing: £6.00
Child Seating: £8.00 and £9.00
Programme Price: £1.70

DISABLED INFORMATION

Wheelchairs: 6 spaces each for Home and Away fans in front of the Main Stand
Helpers: One helper admitted per disabled person
Prices: Concessionary prices for the disabled and helpers
Disabled Toilets: None
Are Bookings Necessary: Yes
Contact: (01625) 264686

Travelling Supporters' Information:
Routes: From the North: Exit the M6 at Junction 19 to Knutsford, follow the A537 to Macclesfield. Follow signs for the Town Centre, then for A523 to Leek. The ground is 1 mile out of the Town Centre on the right; From the South: Exit the M6 at Junction 17 for Sandbach and follow the A534 to Congleton. Then take the A536 to Macclesfield. After passing The Rising Sun on the left, ¼ mile further on turn right after the Texaco Garage (Moss Lane). Following this lane will bring you back to the ground.

MANCHESTER CITY FC

Founded: 1887 (**Entered League:** 1892)
Former Names: Ardwick FC (1897-94)
Nickname: 'Citizens' 'City' 'Blues'
Ground: Maine Road, Moss Side,
Manchester   M14 7WN
Record Attendance: 84,569 (3/3/34)
Pitch Size: 117 × 76 yards

Colours: Shirts – Laser Blue
           Shorts – White
Telephone Nº: (0161) 224-5000
Ticket Office: (0161) 226-2224
Credit Card Bookings: (0161) 227-9229
Fax Number: (0161) 248-8449
Ground Capacity: 33,140 (All seats)

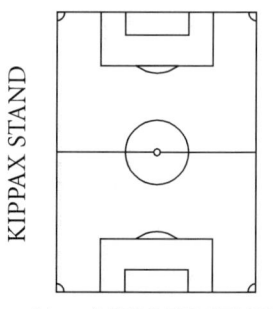

PLATT LANE STAND

KIPPAX STAND

MAINE ROAD
MAIN STAND

(Away) NORTH STAND
(CLAREMONT ROAD)

GENERAL INFORMATION

Supporters Club: c/o Frank Horrocks, Manchester City Supporters' Club, Maine Road, Manchester
Telephone Nº: (0161) 226-5047
Car Parking: Street Parking and Local Schools
Coach Parking: Kippax Street car park
Nearest Railway Station: Manchester Piccadilly (2½ miles)
Nearest Bus Station: Chorlton Street
Club Shop: At Ground and Arndale Centre
Opening Times: Monday to Saturday 9.00am – 5.00pm and Matchdays 9.00am – 6.00pm
Telephone Nº: (0161) 232-1111 (Ground); (0161) 834-4609 (Arndale Centre)
Postal Sales: Yes
Nearest Police Station: Platt Lane, Moss Side
Police Telephone Nº: (0161) 872-5050

GROUND INFORMATION

Away Supporters' Entrances & Sections:
North Stand turnstiles 41-46

ADMISSION INFO (1998/99 PRICES)

Adult Seating: £10.00 – £16.00
Child Seating: £6.00
Note: Prices vary depending on the game category
Programme Price: £1.70

DISABLED INFORMATION

Wheelchairs: 75 spaces for Home and Away fans in the disabled sections, Umbro Stand & Kippax Stand
Helpers: One helper admitted per wheelchair
Prices: Free of charge for disabled. Helpers £5.00
Disabled Toilets: Available in the disabled sections Hospital commentaries are available for 11 blind fans + helpers – in the Main Stand, G Block
Are Bookings Necessary: Yes
Contact: (0161) 226-2224

Travelling Supporters' Information:
Routes: From North & West: Take M61 & M63 exit Junction 9 following Manchester signs (A5103). Turn right at crossroads (2¾ miles) into Claremont Road. After ¼ mile turn left into Maine Road. After ¼ mile turn left into Maine Road; From South: Exit M6 Junction 19 to A556 and M56 Junction 3 following Manchester signs (A5103) (then as North); From East: Exit M62 onto M602 Salford Motorway. Follow to end then take right hand lane and continue into Manchester along A57. Pass Sainsburys and go under railway bridge heading for Mancunian Way. After 2 roundabouts join Mancunian Way (elevated road) but leave at first exit and go under elevated section to roundabout then straight across. Follow road along past Dental Hospital into Lloyd Street and continue along to the ground.

MANCHESTER UNITED FC

Founded: 1878 (**Entered League:** 1892)	**Colours:** Shirts – Red
Former Names: Newton Heath LYR FC	Shorts – White
(1878-92); Newton Heath FC (1892-1902)	**Telephone Nº:** (0161) 930-1968/872-1661
Nickname: 'Red Devils'	**Ticket Office:** (0161) 872-0199
Ground: Sir Matt Busby Way,	**Fax Number:** (0161) 876-5502
Old Trafford, Manchester M16 0RA	**Pitch Size:** 115 × 76 yards
Record Attendance: 76,962 (25/3/39)	**Ground Capacity:** 55,300 (All seats)

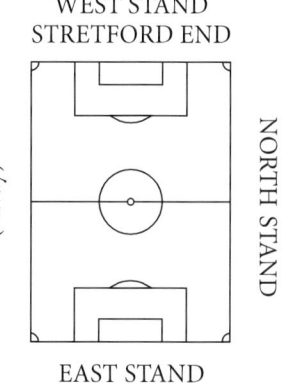

WEST STAND
STRETFORD END

SOUTH STAND (Away)

NORTH STAND

EAST STAND

GENERAL INFORMATION

Supporters Club: Barry Moorhouse, c/o The Club
Telephone Nº: (0161) 872-5208
Car Parking: Lancashire Cricket Ground (1,200 cars)
Coach Parking: By Police direction
Nearest Railway Station: At the ground
Nearest Bus Station: Chorlton Street
Nearest Metro Station: Old Trafford
Club Shops: At the ground
Opening Times: Weekdays 9.00am – 5.00pm;
Matchdays 9.00am to kick-off + 1 hour after match;
Sundays 10.00am – 4.00pm; Non-match Saturdays
9.00am – 5.00pm
Telephone Nº: (0161) 872-3398
Postal Sales: Yes – Merchandising (0161) 877-6077
Nearest Police Stat'n: Talbot Road, Stretford (½ ml)
Police Telephone Nº: (0161) 872-5050

GROUND INFORMATION

Away Supporters' Entrances & Sections:
South Stand (turnstile 22) & East Stand (turnstile 30)

ADMISSION INFO (1998/99 PRICES)

Adult Seating: £14.00 – £20.00
Child Seating: £7.00 – £10.00
Programme Price: £2.00

DISABLED INFORMATION

Wheelchairs: 70 spaces in total for Home and Away
fans in the disabled section – in front of 'L' Stand
Helpers: One helper admitted per disabled person
Prices: Free of charge for Disabled and Helpers
Disabled Toilets: Located near the disabled section
Commentaries are available for the blind
Are Bookings Necessary: Yes
Contact: (0161) 930-1968

Travelling Supporters' Information:
Routes: From North and West: Take M61 to M60 and exit Junction 4 following Manchester (A5081) signs. Turn right after 2½ miles into Sir Matt Busby Way for the ground; From South: Exit M6 at Junction 19 and take Stockport (A556) road then Altrincham (A56). From Altrincham follow Manchester signs and turn left into Sir Matt Busby Way after 6 miles; From East: Exit M62 at Junction 17 and take A56 to Manchester. Follow signs for the South then signs for Chester (Chester Road). Turn right into Sir Matt Busby Way after 2 miles.

MANSFIELD TOWN FC

Founded: 1897 (**Entered League**: 1931)
Former Names: Mansfield Wesleyans FC
(1897-1905)
Nickname: 'Stags'
Ground: Field Mill Ground, Quarry
Lane, Mansfield, Notts.
Record Attendance: 24,467 (10/1/53)

Colours: Shirts – Amber & Royal Blue Stripes
Shorts – Amber & Royal Blue Stripe
Telephone Nº: (01623) 623567
Ticket Office: (01623) 623567
Fax Number: (01623) 625014
Pitch Size: 115 × 70 yards
Ground Capacity: 6,905
Seating Capacity: 2,275

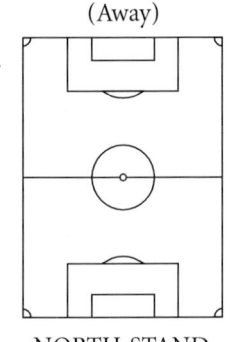

QUARRY LANE
(Away)

BISHOP STREET STAND
(Away)
(Disabled)

WEST STAND

NORTH STAND

GENERAL INFORMATION

Supporters Club: c/o Miss T. Brown, 55 Rosecroft
Drive, Edwards Lane Estate, Nottingham
Telephone Nº: –
Car Parking: Large car park at the ground
Coach Parking: Adjacent to the ground
Nearest Railway Station: Mansfield (5 mins. walk)
Nearest Bus Station: Mansfield
Club Shop: At Ground
Opening Times: Weekdays 9.00am – 5.00pm and
Matchdays 10.00am – 3.00pm and 4.30pm – 5.30pm
Telephone Nº: (01623) 658070
Postal Sales: Yes
Nearest Police Station: Mansfield (¼ mile)
Police Telephone Nº: (01623) 420999

GROUND INFORMATION

Away Supporters' Entrances & Sections:
Quarry Lane turnstiles for Quarry Lane End (open)

ADMISSION INFO (1998/99 PRICES)

Adult Standing: £8.00
Adult Seating: £10.00
Child Standing: £3.00
Child Seating: £5.00
Programme Price: £1.50

DISABLED INFORMATION

Wheelchairs: 40 spaces in total accommodated in
the disabled section – North End of Bishop Street
Helpers: Admitted
Prices: Free for the disabled. Helpers £5.00
Disabled Toilets: Adjacent to the disabled section
Are Bookings Necessary: Not usually
Contact: (01623) 623567

Travelling Supporters' Information:
Routes: From North: Exit M1 at Junction 29 and take A617 to Mansfield. After 6¼ miles turn right at the Leisure Centre into Rosemary Street. Carry on to Quarry Lane and turn right; From South and West: Exit M1 at Junction 28 and take A38 to Mansfield. After 6½ miles turn right at the crossroads into Belvedere Street then turn right after ¼ mile into Quarry Lane; From East: Take A617 to Rainworth, turn left at the crossroads after 3 miles into Windsor Road and turn right at the end into Nottingham Road, then left into Quarry Lane.

MIDDLESBROUGH FC

Founded: 1876 (**Entered League**: 1892)
Former Names: None
Nickname: 'Boro'
Ground: Cellnet Riverside Stadium, Middlesbrough   TS6 3RS
Record Attendance: 30,215 (19/10/96)
Pitch Size: 115 × 75 yards

Colours: Shirts – Red with White Yoke
Shorts – White
Telephone Nº: (01642) 877700
Ticket Office: (01642) 877745
Fax Number: (01642) 877840
Ground Capacity: 35,000 (All seats)

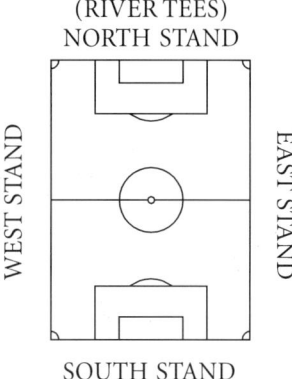

(RIVER TEES)
NORTH STAND

WEST STAND

EAST STAND

SOUTH STAND

GENERAL INFORMATION

Supporters Club: Simon Bolton, c/o The Club
Telephone Nº: (01642) 470512
Car Parking: 1,250 spaces (Season Ticket holders only)
Coach Parking: At the ground
Nearest Railway Station: Middlesbrough (¼ mile)
Nearest Bus Station: Middlesbrough
Club Shops: At Ground and Cleveland Centre
Opening Times: Weekdays 9.30am – 5.00pm; Saturday Matchdays 9.30am – 2.30pm
Cleveland Centre: Monday to Saturday 9.00–5.30pm
Telephone Nº: (01642) 877720 (Ground)
Postal Sales: Yes
Nearest Police Station: Dunning Street (1 mile)
Police Telephone Nº: (01642) 248184

GROUND INFORMATION

Away Supporters' Entrances & Sections:
South Stand turnstiles for the South Stand

ADMISSION INFO (1998/99 PRICES)

Adult Seating: £12.50 – £20.00
Child Seating: £7.00 – £10.00
Programme Price: £1.50

DISABLED INFORMATION

Wheelchairs: 170 spaces in total for home and away fans in the disabled areas, West and South Stands
Helpers: One helper admitted per disabled person
Prices: Telephone the ticket office for prices
Disabled Toilets: Available in West & South Stands
Commentaries are available – 40 headsets
Are Bookings Necessary: Yes
Contact: (01642) 877700

Travelling Supporters' Information:
Routes: From North: Take A19 across flyover and join A66 (Eastbound). At the end of the flyover, turn left at North Ormesby roundabout. The ground is 200 metres down the road; From South: Take A1 and A19 to the junction with A66 (Eastbound). After the flyover, turn left at the North Ormesby roundabout.

MILLWALL FC

Founded: 1885 (**Entered League**: 1920)	**Colours**: Shirts – Blue
Former Names: Millwall Rovers FC (1885-	Shorts – White
93); Millwall Athletic FC (1893-1925)	**Telephone Nº**: (0171) 232-1222
Nickname: 'Lions'	**Ticket Office**: (0171) 231-9999
Ground: The Den, Zampa Road,	**Fax Number**: (0171) 231-3663
London SE16 3LN	**Pitch Size**: 112 × 74 yards
Record Attendance: 20,093 (10/1/94)	**Ground Capacity**: 20,146 (All seats)

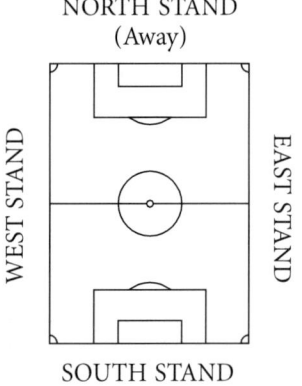

NORTH STAND
(Away)

WEST STAND

EAST STAND

SOUTH STAND

GENERAL INFORMATION
Supporters Club: Yes – c/o Club
Telephone Nº: (0171) 232-1222
Car Parking: Street Parking
Coach Parking: Adjacent to ground
Nearest Railway Station: New Cross Gate/South Bermondsey (½ mile)
Nearest Tube Station: New Cross Gate (1 mile); Surrey Quays (½ mile)
Club Shop: Next to Stadium
Opening Times: Daily 9.30am – 4.30pm
Telephone Nº: (0171) 231-9845
Postal Sales: Yes
Nearest Police Station: Deptford/Lewisham (1 mile)
Police Telephone Nº: (0171) 679-9217

GROUND INFORMATION
Away Supporters' Entrances & Sections:
North East Stand turnstiles 31-36 for North Stand

ADMISSION INFO (1998/99 PRICES)
Adult Seating: £11.00 – £15.00
Child Seating: £5.00
Programme Price: £1.80

DISABLED INFORMATION
Wheelchairs: 200 spaces in total for home and away fans in the disabled section, West Stand
Helpers: One helper admitted per disabled person
Prices: Free of charge for disabled. Helpers £11.00
Disabled Toilets: 17 toilets available around the Stadium
Commentaries are available for the blind
Are Bookings Necessary: Yes
Contact: (0171) 232-1222

Travelling Supporters' Information:
Routes: From North: Follow City signs from M1/A1 then signs for Shoreditch & Whitechapel. Follow Ring Road signs for Dover, cross over Tower Bridge and after 1 mile take 1st exit at the roundabout onto A2. From Elephant and Castle take A2 (New Kent Road) into Old Kent Road and turn left after 4 miles at Canterbury Arms pub into Ilderton Road then follow Surrey Canal Road to Zampa Road; From South: Take A20 & A21 following signs to London. At New Cross follow signs for Stadium; From East: Take A2 to New Cross (then as South); From West: From M4 & M3 follow South Circular (A205) then follow signs for Clapham, City (A3) then Camberwell to New Cross and then as from the South.

NEWCASTLE UNITED FC

Founded: 1882 (**Entered League**: 1893)	**Colours**: Shirts – Black and White Stripes
Former Names: Newcastle East End FC	Shorts – Black
(1882-92) joined Newcastle West End FC	**Telephone N°**: (0191) 201-8400
Nickname: 'Magpies'	**Ticket Office**: (0191) 261-1571
Ground: St. James Park, Newcastle-	**Fax Number**: (0191) 201-8600
Upon-Tyne NE1 4ST	**Pitch Size**: 110 × 73 yards
Record Attendance: 68,386 (3/9/30)	**Ground Capacity**: 36,834 (All seats)

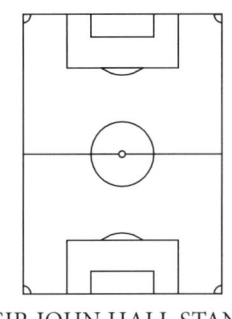

STRAWBERRY PLACE
EXHIBITION STAND

ST. JAMES STREET EAST STAND

BARRACK ROAD MILBURN STAND

SIR JOHN HALL STAND

GENERAL INFORMATION

Supporters Club: None
Telephone N°: –
Car Parking: Street Parking
Coach Parking: By Police direction
Nearest Railway Station: Newcastle Central (¼ ml)
Nearest Bus Station: Gallowgate (¼ mile)
Club Shop: At ground, Eldon Square, MetroCentre & Monument Mall
Opening Times: All shops are open Monday to Saturday 9.00am – 5.00pm; Eldon open until 8.00pm on Thursdays; MetroCentre open until at least 7.00pm Monday to Saturday
Telephone N°: (0191) 201-8426
Postal Sales: Yes **Phone**: (0990) 501892
Nearest Police Station: Market Street, Newcastle
Police Telephone N°: (0191) 232-3451

GROUND INFORMATION

Away Supporters' Entrances & Sections:
North East Corner for Sir John Hall Stand

ADMISSION INFO (1998/99 PRICES)

Adult Seating: £15.00 – £25.00
Child Seating: £7.00 – £16.00
Programme Price: £1.50
Note: It is expected than only Season Ticket holders will be admitted in 1998/99

DISABLED INFORMATION

Wheelchairs: 95 spaces in total in the disabled areas, Sir John Hall Stand and Exhibition Stand
Helpers: One helper admitted per disabled person
Prices: Prices available on application
Disabled Toilets: Available in Sir John Hall Stand
Commentaries are available for 20 blind supporters
Are Bookings Necessary: Yes
Contact: (0191) 261-1571

Travelling Supporters' Information:
Routes: From North: Follow A1 into Newcastle, then Hexham signs into Percy Street. Turn right into Leazes Park Road; From South: Take A1M, then after Birtley Granada Services take A69 Gateshead Western Bypass (bear left on Motorway). Follow Airport signs for approx. 3 miles then take A692 (Newcastle) sign, crossing the Redheugh Bridge. At roundabout, take 3rd exit (Blenheim Street). Proceed over two sets of traffic lights crossing Westmorland Road, Westgate Road then left into Bath Lane. Over traffic lights to roundabout and take 3rd exit into Barrack Road; From West: Take A69 towards City Centre. Pass Newcastle General Hospital. At traffic lights after Hospital turn left into Brighton Grove. After 70 yards turn right into Stanhope Street, proceed into Barrack Road.

NORTHAMPTON TOWN FC

Founded: 1897 (**Entered League**: 1920)	**Colours**: Shirts – Claret and White
Former Names: None	Shorts – White
Nickname: 'Cobblers'	**Telephone Nº**: (01604) 757773
Ground: Sixfields Stadium, Upton Way,	**Ticket Office**: (01604) 588338
Northampton NN5 5QA	**Fax Number**: (01604) 751613
Record Attendance: 7,501 (13/5/98)	**Ground Capacity**: 7,653 (All seats)
Pitch Size: 112 × 75 yards	

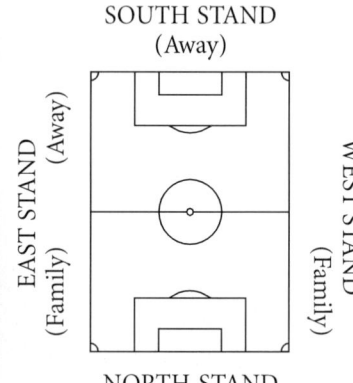

SOUTH STAND
(Away)

EAST STAND
(Away)

EAST STAND
(Family)

WEST STAND
(Family)

NORTH STAND

GENERAL INFORMATION

Supporters Club: Northampton Supporters Trust, 10 Ainsdale Close, Links View, Northampton
Telephone Nº: –
Car Parking: At the ground
Coach Parking: At the ground
Nearest Railway Station: Northampton Castle (2 miles)
Nearest Bus Station: Greyfriars
Club Shop: At Ground
Opening Times: Weekdays 10.00am – 4.00pm and Matchdays 9.00am – 6.00pm
Telephone Nº: (01604) 757773
Postal Sales: Yes
Nearest Police Station: Campbell Square, Northampton
Police Telephone Nº: (01604) 700700

GROUND INFORMATION

Away Supporters' Entrances & Sections:
South Stand Entrance for South and East Stands

ADMISSION INFO (1998/99 PRICES)

Adult Seating: £10.50 – £13.50
Child Seating: £6.00 – £9.50
Programme Price: £1.50
In addition to various combinations of adults and children, concessions also apply

DISABLED INFORMATION

Wheelchairs: 80 spaces in total for Home and Away fans in various areas of the ground
Helpers: One helper admitted per disabled person
Prices: £6.00 each for disabled fans and helpers
Disabled Toilets: Available by the disabled areas
Commentaries are available for the blind
Are Bookings Necessary: Yes
Contact: (01604) 588338

Travelling Supporters' Information:
Routes: From All Parts: Exit the M1 at Junction 15A following the signs for Sixfields Leisure onto Upton Way – the ground is approximately 2 miles.

NORWICH CITY FC

Founded: 1902 (**Entered League**: 1920)	**Colours**: Shirts – Yellow
Former Names: None	Shorts – Yellow
Nickname: 'Canaries'	**Telephone Nº**: (01603) 760760
Ground: Carrow Road, Norwich	**Ticket Office**: (01603) 761661
NR1 1JE	**Fax Number**: (01603) 613886
Record Attendance: 43,984 (30/3/63)	**Ground Capacity**: 21,972 (All seats)
Pitch Size: 114 × 74 yards	

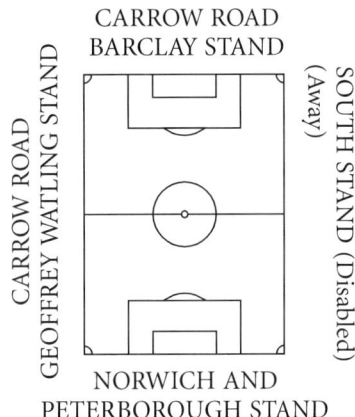

CARROW ROAD
BARCLAY STAND

CARROW ROAD
GEOFFREY WATLING STAND

SOUTH STAND (Disabled)
(Away)

NORWICH AND
PETERBOROUGH STAND

GENERAL INFORMATION

Supporters Club: c/o Ros Watson, Carrow Road, Norwich
Telephone Nº: (01603) 218714
Car Parking: City Centre car parks (nearby)
Coach Parking: Lower Clarence Road
Nearest Railway Station: Norwich Thorpe (1 mile)
Nearest Bus Station: Surrey Street, Norwich
Club Shop: In City Stand
Opening Times: Weekdays and Matchdays 9.00am – 5.00pm
Telephone Nº: (01603) 218711
Postal Sales: Yes
Nearest Police Stat'n: Bethel Street, Norwich (1 ml)
Police Telephone Nº: (01603) 768769

GROUND INFORMATION

Away Supporters' Entrances & Sections:
Turnstiles 1-3 – Barclay End for South Stand Blocks F, G, H and J

ADMISSION INFO (1998/99 PRICES)

Adult Seating: £9.00 – £25.00
Child Seating: £1.00 – £11.00
Programme Price: £2.00
Note: Prices vary according to the category of the game

DISABLED INFORMATION

Wheelchairs: 34 spaces for home fans and 6 for away fans in South Stand/River End corner
Helpers: One helper admitted per disabled person
Prices: Free of charge for disabled. Helpers £7.00 – £11.00 according to match category
Disabled Toilets: One available within disabled area
Are Bookings Necessary: Yes
Contact: (01603) 761661

Travelling Supporters' Information:
Routes: From South: Take A11 or A140 and turn right onto A47 towards Great Yarmouth & Lowestoft, take A146 Norwich/Lowestoft sliproad, turn left towards Norwich and follow road signs for the Football Ground; From West: Take A47 on to A146 Norwich/Lowestoft slip road. Turn left towards Norwich, follow the road signs for the Football Ground.

NOTTINGHAM FOREST FC

Founded: 1865 (**Entered League:** 1892)
Former Names: None
Nickname: 'Reds'; 'Forest'
Ground: City Ground, Nottingham,
NG2 5FJ
Record Attendance: 49,945 (28/10/67)
Pitch Size: 115 × 78 yards

Colours: Shirts – Red
            Shorts – White
Telephone Nº: (0115) 982-4444
Ticket Office: (0115) 982-4445
Fax Number: (0115) 982-4455
Ground Capacity: 30,602 (All seats)

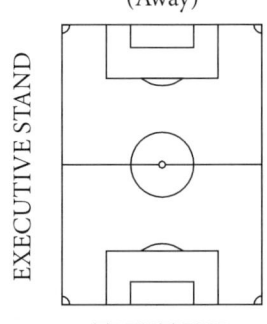

BRIDGFORD STAND
(Away)

EXECUTIVE STAND

PAVILION ROAD
MAIN STAND

TRENT END
STAND

GENERAL INFORMATION

Supporters Club: Mr. B. Elvidge, c/o The Club
Telephone Nº: (0115) 982-4444
Car Parking: East car park (300 cars) & street parking
Coach Parking: East car park, Meadow Lane
Nearest Railway Station: Nottingham Midland (½ mile)
Nearest Bus Station: Victoria Street/Broadmarsh Centre
Club Shop: At Ground
Opening Times: Weekdays 9.00am – 5.00pm; Matchdays 9.00am – 3.00pm
Telephone Nº: (0115) 982-4447
Postal Sales: Yes
Nearest Police Station: Rectory Road, West Bridgford (1 mile)
Police Telephone Nº: (0115) 948-1888

GROUND INFORMATION

Away Supporters' Entrances & Sections:
Entrances via East car park for Bridgford Stand

ADMISSION INFO (1998/99 PRICES)

Adult Seating: £12.00 – £28.00
Child Seating: £6.00 – £14.00
Note: Prices vary depending on the match category
Programme Price: £2.00

DISABLED INFORMATION

Wheelchairs: 50 spaces in total for Home and Away fans in the disabled area, in front of Executive Stand
Helpers: One helper admitted per disabled person
Prices: Free of charge for disabled. Helpers £12.00
Disabled Toilets: Available in the Executive Stand
Are Bookings Necessary: Yes
Contact: (0115) 982-4445

Travelling Supporters' Information:
Routes: From North: Exit M1 at Junction 26 following Nottingham signs (A610) then Melton Mowbray an Trent Bridge (A606) signs. Cross River Trent, left into Radcliffe Road then left into Colwick Road for ground; From South: Exit M1 at Junction 24 following signs for Nottingham (South) to Trent Bridge. Turn right into Radcliffe Road then left into Colwick Road; From East: Take A52 to West Bridgford, turn right into Colwick Road; From West: Take A52 into Nottingham following signs for Melton Mowbray and Trent Bridge, cross Rover Trent (then as North).

NOTTS COUNTY FC

Founded: 1862 (**Entered League:** 1888)
Former Names: None
Nickname: 'Magpies'
Ground: Meadow Lane, Nottingham, NG2 3HJ
Record Attendance: 47,310 (12/3/55)
Pitch Size: 117 × 76 yards

Colours: Shirts – Black and White Stripes
Shorts – Black
Telephone Nº: (0115) 952-9000
Ticket Office: (0115) 955-7210
Fax Number: (0115) 955-3994
Ground Capacity: 20,300 (All seats)

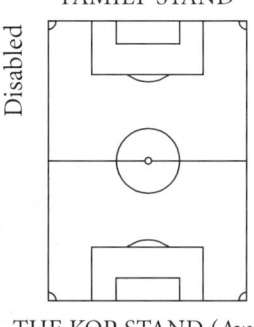

MEADOW LANE
FAMILY STAND

JIMMY SIRRELL STAND
Disabled

DEREK PAVIS
STAND

THE KOP STAND (Away)
CATTLE MARKET ROAD

GENERAL INFORMATION

Supporters Club: I. Mills, c/o The Club
Telephone Nº: (0115) 955-7255
Car Parking: British Waterways, Meadow Lane
Coach Parking: Incinerator Road (Cattle Market Corner)
Nearest Railway Station: Nottingham Midland (½ mile)
Nearest Bus Station: Broadmarsh Centre
Club Shop: At Ground
Opening Times: Fridays and Matchdays 9.00am – 5.00pm
Telephone Nº: (0115) 952-9000
Postal Sales: Yes
Nearest Police Station: Station Street, Nottingham
Police Telephone Nº: (0115) 948-1888

GROUND INFORMATION

Away Supporters' Entrances & Sections:
Cattle Market Corner for The Kop Stand

ADMISSION INFO (1998/99 PRICES)

Adult Seating: £11.00 – £15.00
Child Seating: £5.50 – £7.50
Senior Citizens: £6.00 – £10.00
Programme Price: £1.80

DISABLED INFORMATION

Wheelchairs: 100 spaces in total in the disabled area, County Road/Meadow Lane End corner
Helpers: One helper admitted per disabled fan
Prices: Free for wheelchair disabled.
Disabled Toilets: Available next to the disabled area
Are Bookings Necessary: Yes
Contact: (0115) 955-7210

Travelling Supporters' Information:
Routes: From North: Exit M1 Junction 26 following Nottingham signs (A610) then Melton Mowbray and Trent Bridge (A606) signs. Before River Trent turn left into Meadow Lane; From South: Exit M1 Junction 24 following signs Nottingham (South) to Trent Bridge, cross River and follow one-way system to the right, then turn left and right at traffic lights then second right into Meadow Lane; From East: Take A52 to West Bridgford/Trent Bridge, cross River and follow one-way system to the right then turn left and right at traffic lights, then second right into Meadow Lane; From West: Take A52 into Nottingham following signs for Melton Mowbray and Trent Bridge, before River Trent turn left into Meadow Lane.

OLDHAM ATHLETIC FC

Founded: 1895 (**Entered League:** 1907)
Former Names: Pine Villa FC (1895-99)
Nickname: 'Latics'
Ground: Boundary Park, Oldham, OL1 2PA
Record Attendance: 47,671 (25/1/30)
Pitch Size: 110 × 78 yards

Colours: Shirts – Royal Blue
Shorts – Royal Blue
Telephone Nº: (0161) 624-4972 (24 hrs)
Ticket Office: (0161) 624-4972
Fax Number: (0161) 627-5915
Ground Capacity: 13,700 (All seats)

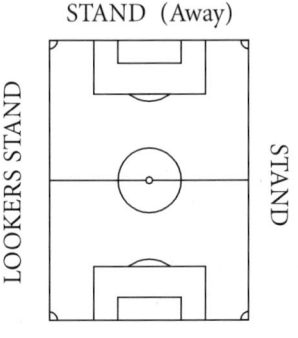

ELLEN GROUP STAND (Away)

LOOKERS STAND

GEORGE HILL STAND

SETON STAND

GENERAL INFORMATION
Supporters Club: Dave Cunningham, c/o The Club
Telephone Nº: (0161) 624-4972
Car Parking: Lookers Stand car park (1,000 cars)
Coach Parking: At the ground
Nearest Railway Station: Oldham Werneth (1½ ml)
Nearest Bus Station: Oldham Centre (2 miles)
Club Shop: At Ground
Opening Times: Mondays to Fridays 9.00am to 5.00pm. Saturdays 9.00am to 3.00pm
Telephone Nº: (0161) 652-0966
Postal Sales: Yes
Nearest Police Station: Chadderton
Police Telephone Nº: (0161) 624-0444

GROUND INFORMATION
Away Supporters' Entrances & Sections:
Ellen Group Stand turnstiles for seating

ADMISSION INFO (1998/99 PRICES)
Adult Seating: £7.50 – £13.00 (Away fans £12.00)
Child Seating: £5.00 (Away fans £5.00)
Programme Price: £1.60

DISABLED INFORMATION
Wheelchairs: 36 spaces in total in the disabled areas, Lookers Paddock, Seton & Rochdale Road Stands
Helpers: One helper admitted per disabled person
Prices: Free for the disabled. Helpers full price
Disabled Toilets: In Lookers Paddock and Rochdale Road Stand
Are Bookings Necessary: Yes
Contact: (0161) 624-4972

Travelling Supporters' Information:
Routes: From All Parts: Exit M62 at Junction 20 and take A627M to junction with the A664. Take the 1st exit at roundabout on to Broadway, then 1st right into Hilbre Avenue which leads to the car park.

OXFORD UNITED FC

Founded: 1893 (**Entered League:** 1962)	**Colours:** Shirts – Yellow with navy trim
Former Names: Headington United FC	Shorts – Navy with yellow trim
(1893-1960)	**Telephone Nº:** (01865) 761503
Nickname: 'U's'	**Ticket Office:** (01865) 761503
Ground: Manor Ground, London Road,	**Fax Number:** (01865) 741820
Headington, Oxford OX3 7RS	**Pitch Size:** 110 × 75 yards
Record Attendance: 22,730 (29/2/64)	**Ground Capacity:** 9,572
New ground currently under construction	**Seating Capacity:** 2,777

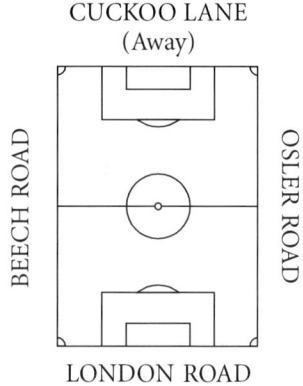

CUCKOO LANE
(Away)

BEECH ROAD

OSLER ROAD

LONDON ROAD

GENERAL INFORMATION
Supporters Club: Gary Whiting, c/o The Club
Telephone Nº: (01865) 763063
Car Parking: Street Parking
Coach Parking: Off Headley Way in Franklin Road
Nearest Railway Station: Oxford (3 miles)
Nearest Bus Station: Queen's Lane (2 miles)
Club Shop: The United Experience, Headington
Opening Times: Monday to Friday 10.00 – 5.00pm;
Saturdays 10am – 4.00pm (Matchdays until 2.45pm)
Telephone Nº: (01865) 761503
Postal Sales: Yes
Nearest Police Station: Cowley (2 miles)
Police Telephone Nº: (01865) 749909

GROUND INFORMATION
Away Supporters' Entrances & Sections:
Cuckoo Lane turnstiles 5-11 for Cuckoo Lane End

ADMISSION INFO (1998/99 PRICES)
Adult Standing: £9.50 – £11.00
Adult Seating: £9.50 – £14.00
Child Standing: £5.50 – £6.50
Child Seating: £4.50 – £9.50
Programme Price: £1.70

DISABLED INFORMATION
Wheelchairs: 25 spaces in total for Home and Away
fans in the disabled section, Beech Road Corner
Helpers: One helper admitted per disabled person
Prices: £5.50 for disabled. Helpers normal prices
Disabled Toilets: Available in Beech Road corner
Are Bookings Necessary: Yes
Contact: (01865) 761503

Travelling Supporters' Information:
Routes: From North: Exit M40 at Junction 9. Follow signs to Oxford (A34). Take slip road A44 marked Witney, Woodstock. At roundabout take 1st exit (Pear Tree). Follow to next roundabout A44 junction with A40 Woodstock Road, take 2nd exit marked A40 London. Down to next roundabout (Banbury Road), take 2nd exit to Northern by-pass. Cars take next left turn at slip road marked New Marston ½ mile and JR Hospital 1 mile. (Coaches follow diversions to avoid weak bridge, next roundabout A40 (Green Road), take 5th exit, follow signs for A40 junction with B4105 Marston). Down to mini-roundabout and turn left. Straight up Headley Way, coaches should take 2nd junction right marked Franklin Road (leads to Coach Park). Cars – side street parking only. Take care for matchday parking restrictions; From South: A34 by-pass to Junction A44 Pear Tree (then as North); From East: Cars and coaches follow diversion directions a from Green Road roundabout; From West: Take A34 following signs to M40. Take exit A44 marked Woodstock, take 3rd exit (Pear Tree), then as North.

PETERBOROUGH UNITED FC

<table>
<tr><td>

Founded: 1934 (**Entered League**: 1960)
Former Names: None
Nickname: 'Posh'
Ground: London Road, Peterborough,
Cambs. PE2 8AL
Record Attendance: 30,096 (20/2/65)
Pitch Size: 112 × 71 yards

</td><td>

Colours: Shirts – Blue
         Shorts – White
Telephone Nº: (01733) 563947
Ticket Office: (01733) 563947
Fax Number: (01733) 557210
Ground Capacity: 15,656
Seating Capacity: 9,576

</td></tr>
</table>

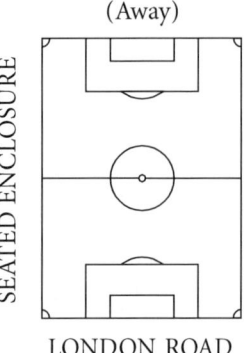

MOYS END
(Away)

MAIN STAND
SEATED ENCLOSURE

FREEMANS FAMILY
STAND

LONDON ROAD

GENERAL INFORMATION
Supporters Club: Barry Bennett, c/o Club
Telephone Nº: (01733) 703658
Car Parking: Ample parking at the ground
Coach Parking: At the rear of the ground
Nearest Railway Station: Peterborough (1 mile)
Nearest Bus Station: Peterborough (1 mile)
Club Shop: At Ground
Opening Times: Monday – Friday 9.00am – 5.00pm
Telephone Nº: (01733) 569760
Postal Sales: Yes
Nearest Police Station: Bridge Street, Peterborough
(5 minutes walk)
Police Telephone Nº: (01733) 563232

GROUND INFORMATION
Away Supporters' Entrances & Sections:
Turnstile A, Moys End for Block A Seating

ADMISSION INFO (1998/99 PRICES)
Adult Standing: £7.00
Adult Seating: £9.00 – £10.00
Child Standing: £3.00 (Home fans only)
Child Seating: £3.00
Programme Price: £1.50

DISABLED INFORMATION
Wheelchairs: 40 spaces in total for Home and Away
fans in disabled area, right side of Freemans Stand
Helpers: One helper admitted per disabled person
Prices: Half the price of seating areas for disabled
and helpers
Disabled Toilets: In the Freemans Family Stand
Are Bookings Necessary: Yes
Contact: (01733) 563947

Travelling Supporters' Information:
Routes: From North and West: Take A1 then A47 into the Town Centre and follow Whittlesey signs across the
river into London Road; From East: Take A47 into the Town Centre (then as North); From South: Take A1
then A15 into London Road.

PLYMOUTH ARGYLE FC

Founded: 1886 (**Entered League:** 1920)	**Telephone Nº:** (01752) 562561
Former Names: Argyle FC (1886-1903)	**Ticket Office:** (01752) 562561
Nickname: 'Pilgrims'; 'Argyle'	**Fax Number:** (01752) 606167
Ground: Home Park, Plymouth PL2 3DQ	**Pitch Size:** 112 × 72 yards
Record Attendance: 43,596 (10/10/36)	**Ground Capacity:** 19,900
Colours: Shirts – Green with Black Band	**Seating Capacity:** 6,700
Shorts – Black	

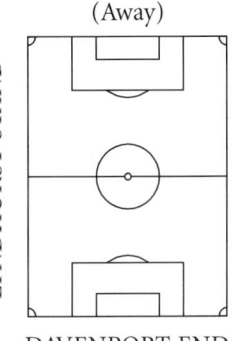

BARN PARK END
(Away)

TAVISTOCK ROAD
LYNDHURST STAND

GRAND STAND
MAYFLOWER ENCLOSURE

DAVENPORT END

GENERAL INFORMATION

Supporters Club: S. Rendell, c/o Club
Telephone Nº: (01752) 562561
Car Parking: Car park for 1,000 cars is adjacent
Coach Parking: Central Car Park
Nearest Railway Station: Plymouth North Road
Nearest Bus Station: Bretonside, Plymouth
Club Shop: At the ground
Opening Times: Monday to Saturday 9.00am –
5.00pm (closed during matches)
Telephone Nº: (01752) 558292
Postal Sales: Yes
Nearest Police Station: Devonport (1 mile)
Police Telephone Nº: (01752) 701188

GROUND INFORMATION

Away Supporters' Entrances & Sections:
Barn Park End turnstiles for open accommodation

ADMISSION INFO (1998/99 PRICES)

Adult Standing: £7.50 or £8.00
Adult Seating: £10.00 – £13.00
Child Standing: £6.00 – £6.50
Child Seating: £8.00 – £11.00
Programme Price: £1.50
Note: Special rates for adults and children in the
Family Enclosure (Prices shown are for category 'A'
games – category 'B' and 'C' games will be at a higher
price).

DISABLED INFORMATION

Wheelchairs: 60 spaces in total for Home and Away
fans in the disabled section, Devonport End
Helpers: One helper admitted per disabled person
Prices: Free of charge for disabled. Helpers £6.50
Disabled Toilets: Adjacent to the disabled section
Commentaries are available for the blind
Are Bookings Necessary: Yes
Contact: (01752) 562561

Travelling Supporters' Information:
Routes: From All Parts: Take A38 to Tavistock Road (A386), then branch left following signs for Plymouth
(A386) and continue for 1¼ miles. The car park is on the left (signposted Home Park).

PORTSMOUTH FC

Founded: 1898 (**Entered League**: 1920)
Former Names: None
Nickname: 'Pompey'
Ground: Fratton Park, 57 Frogmore Road, Portsmouth, Hants   PO4 8RA
Record Attendance: 51,385 (26/2/49)

Colours: Shirts – Blue
                  Shorts – White
Telephone Nº: (01705) 731204
Ticket Office: (01705) 750825/618777
Fax Number: (01705) 734129
Pitch Size: 110 × 72 yards
Ground Capacity: 19,300 (All seats)

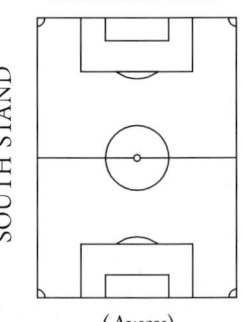

FROGMORE ROAD
FRATTON END

CARISBROOKE ROAD
SOUTH STAND

MILTON LANE
NORTH STAND

(Away)
MILTON END
ASPLEY ROAD

GENERAL INFORMATION

Supporters Club: c/o The Club
Telephone Nº: –
Car Parking: Street Parking
Coach Parking: By Police direction
Nearest Railway Station: Fratton (adjacent)
Nearest Bus Station: Hilsea
Club Shop: At Ground
Opening Times: Weekdays and Saturdays 9.00am to 5.30pm. Saturday Matchdays shuts 3.00pm–4.45pm
Telephone Nº: (01705) 738358
Postal Sales: Yes
Nearest Police Station: Southsea
Police Telephone Nº: (01705) 321111

GROUND INFORMATION

Away Supporters' Entrances & Sections:
Aspley Road – Milton Road side for Aspley Road End

ADMISSION INFO (1998/99 PRICES)

Adult Seating: £12.00 – £16.00
Child Seating: £4.00 – £10.00
Programme Price: £2.00

DISABLED INFORMATION

Wheelchairs: Limited number of spaces available in the disabled section, Fratton End
Helpers: One helper admitted per disabled person
Prices: Free for the disabled. Helpers pay full price
Disabled Toilets: One available in disabled section
Are Bookings Necessary: Yes
Contact: (01705) 731204

Travelling Supporters' Information:
Routes: From North and West: Take M27 and M275 to the end then take the 2nd exit at the roundabout and after ¼ mile turn right at the 'T' junction into London Road (A2047). After 1¼ miles cross the railway bridge and turn left into Goldsmith Avenue. After ½ mile turn left into Frogmore Road; From East: Take A27 following Southsea signs (A2030). Turn left at the roundabout (3 miles) onto A288, then right into Priory Crescent and next right into Carisbrooke Road.

PORT VALE FC

<table>
<tr><td>

Founded: 1876 (**Entered League:** 1892)
Former Names: Burslem Port Vale FC
Nickname: 'Valiants'
Ground: Vale Park, Burslem, Stoke-on-Trent   ST6 1AW
Record Attendance: 49,768 (20/2/60)
Pitch Size: 114 × 77 yards

</td><td>

Colours: Shirts – White
              Shorts – Black
Telephone Nº: (01782) 814134
Ticket Office: (01782) 814134
Fax Number: (01782) 834981
Ground Capacity: 17,616 (All seats)

</td></tr>
</table>

HAMIL ROAD
CAUDWELL STAND
(Away)

LORNE STREET (Disabled)

RAILWAY STAND

BYCARS STAND

GENERAL INFORMATION
Supporters Club: Geoff Davis, c/o Club
Telephone Nº: –
Car Parking: Car parks at the ground
Coach Parking: Hamil Road car park
Nearest Railway Station: Stoke
Nearest Bus Station: Burslem (adjacent)
Club Shop: At Ground
Opening Times: Monday to Saturday 9.00am –
5.30pm
Telephone Nº: (01782) 833545
Postal Sales: Yes
Nearest Police Station: Burslem
Police Telephone Nº: (01782) 577114

GROUND INFORMATION
Away Supporters' Entrances & Sections:
Hamil Road turnstiles for Caudwell Stand

ADMISSION INFO (1998/99 PRICES)
Adult Seating: £12.00 – £15.00
Child Seating: £5.00 – £11.00
(Discounts for child concessions when pre-booked)
Programme Price: £1.80

DISABLED INFORMATION
Wheelchairs: 72 spaces in total in the disabled
section, Lorne Street/Hamil Road Corner
Helpers: One helper admitted per disabled person
Prices: £5.00 for the disabled. £10.00 for helpers
Disabled Toilets: One available in the disabled area
Commentaries are available – please contact the
club for further information
Are Bookings Necessary: Yes
Contact: (01782) 814134

Travelling Supporters' Information:
Routes: From North: Exit M6 at Junction 16 and follow Stoke signs (A500). Branch left off the A500 at the exit signposted Tunstall, take 2nd exit at roundabout into Newcastle Street. Proceed through traffic lights into Moorland Road and take 2nd turning on the left into Hamil Road; From South and West: Exit M6 at Junction 15 and take A5006 and A500. After 6¼ miles branch left (then as North); From East: Take A50 or A52 into Stoke following Burslem signs into Waterloo Road, turn right at Burslem crossroads into Moorland Road (then as North).

PRESTON NORTH END FC

Founded: 1881 (**Entered League:** 1888)
Nickname: 'Lilywhites'; 'North End'
Ground: Deepdale, Preston   PR1 6RU
Record Attendance: 42,684 (23/4/38)
Colours: Shirts – White
              Shorts – Blue

Telephone Nº: (01772) 902020
Ticket Office: (01772) 902000
Fax Number: (01772) 653266
Pitch Size: 110 × 72 yards
Ground Capacity: 21,500
Seating Capacity: 15,000

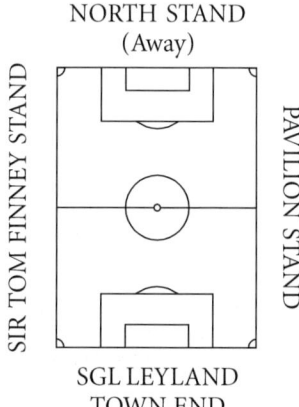

NORTH STAND
(Away)

SIR TOM FINNEY STAND

RED ROSE RADIO
PAVILION STAND

SGL LEYLAND
TOWN END

GENERAL INFORMATION
Supporters Club: c/o The Club
Telephone Nº: –
Car Parking: Sir Tom Finney Car Park, Moor Park and Deepdale Primary School
Coach Parking: Deepdale Retail Park
Nearest Railway Station: Preston (2 miles)
Nearest Bus Station: Preston (1 mile)
Club Shop: At ground, in Town Centre and Leyland
Opening Times: Monday to Saturday 9.00am to 5.00pm
Telephone Nº: (01772) 902040
Postal Sales: Yes
Nearest Police Station: Lawson Street (1 mile)
Police Telephone Nº: (01772) 203203

GROUND INFORMATION
Away Supporters' Entrances & Sections:
North Stand entrances and accommodation

ADMISSION INFO (1998/99 PRICES)
Adult Standing: £9.50 – £10.00
Adult Seating: £12.00 – £13.00
Child Standing: £5.50 – £6.00
Child Seating: £7.00 – £8.00
Programme Price: £1.80

DISABLED INFORMATION
Wheelchairs: 100 spaces available in the Tom Finney Stand, 80 spaces available in the North Stand
Helpers: One helper admitted per wheelchair
Prices: Free for the disabled. Helpers £8.00
Disabled Toilets: Available in Tom Finney Stand and North Stand
Commentaries are available for the blind
Are Bookings Necessary: Usually
Contact: (01772) 902020

Travelling Supporters' Information:
Routes: From North: Take M6 then M55 to Junction 1. Follow signs for Preston A6. After 2 miles turn left at the crossroads into Blackpool Road (A5085). Turn right ¾ mile into Deepdale; From South and East: Exit M6 at Junction 31 and follow Preston signs (A59). Take the 2nd exit at the roundabout (1 mile) into Blackpool Road. Turn left after 1¼ miles into Deepdale; From West: Exit M55 at Junction 1 (then as North).

QUEEN'S PARK RANGERS FC

Founded: 1882 (**Entered League:** 1920)	**Colours:** Shirts – Blue and White Hoops
Former Names: Amalgamation of	Shorts – White
St. Jude's FC & Christchurch Rangers FC	**Telephone Nº:** (0181) 743-0262
Nickname: 'Rangers' 'R's'	**Ticket Office:** (0181) 743-0262
Ground: Rangers Stadium, South Africa	**Fax Number:** (0181) 749-0994
Road, London W12 7PA	**Pitch Size:** 112 × 72 yards
Record Attendance: 35,353 (27/4/74)	**Ground Capacity:** 19,003 (All seats)

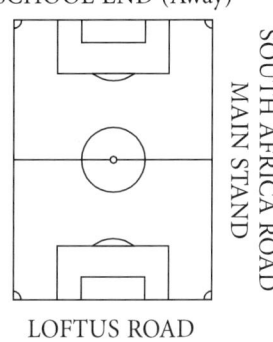

BLOEMFONTEIN ROAD
SCHOOL END (Away)

ELLERSLIE ROAD STAND (Disabled)

SOUTH AFRICA ROAD MAIN STAND

LOFTUS ROAD STAND

GENERAL INFORMATION

Supporters Club: Patricia Dix, c/o The Club
Telephone Nº: (0181) 740-2534
Car Parking: Street Parking
Coach Parking: By Police direction
Nearest Railway Station: Shepherd's Bush
Nearest Tube Station: White City (Central)
Club Shop: At Ground
Opening Times: Monday to Friday 9.00am –
5.00pm;   Saturday 9.00am – 1.00pm
Telephone Nº: (0181) 749-6862
Postal Sales: Yes
Nearest Police Station: Uxbridge Road, Shepherd's
Bush (½ mile)
Police Telephone Nº: (0181) 741-6212

GROUND INFORMATION

Away Supporters' Entrances & Sections:
South Africa Road turnstiles 13-15 & Ellerslie Road
turnstiles 9-12 for School End Stand

ADMISSION INFO (1998/99 PRICES)

Adult Seating: £15.00 – £20.00
Child Seating: £9.00 – £10.00
Programme Price: £1.50
Note: Prices vary depending on the category of the
game. Membership discounts are available

DISABLED INFORMATION

Wheelchairs: 18 spaces in the Wheelchair enclosure,
left side of the Ellerslie Road Stand
Helpers: One helper admitted per wheelchair
Prices: Free of charge for Disabled and Helpers
Disabled Toilets: Available in corner of Ellerslie
Road Stand
Commentaries are available for the blind
Are Bookings Necessary: Yes
Contact: Please contact the club in writing

Travelling Supporters' Information:
Routes: From North: Take M1 & M406 North Circular for Neasden, left after ¾ mile (A404) following signs
Harlesden, Hammersmith, past White City Stadium, right into White City Road, left into South Africa Road; From
South: Take A206, A3 across Putney Bridge follow signs to Hammersmith, Oxford A219 to Shepherd's Bush. Join
A4020 following signs to Acton, turn right (¼ mile) into Loftus Road; From East: Take A12, A406 then A503 to join
Ring Road, follow Oxford signs join A40(M), branch left (2 miles) to M41, 3rd exit at roundabout to A4020 (then as
South); From West: Take M4 to Chiswick then A315 & A402 to Shepherd's Bush, join A4020 (then as South).

READING FC

Founded: 1871 (**Entered League**: 1920)	**Colours**: Shirts – Blue and White Hoops
Former Names: Amalgamated with	Shorts – Blue
Hornets FC (1877) and Earley FC (1889)	**Telephone Nº**: (0118) 968-1100
Nickname: 'Royals'	**Ticket Office**: (0118) 968-1000
Ground: Madejski Stadium, Junction 11	**Fax Number**: (0118) 968-1101
M4, Reading, Berks. RG2 0FL	**Pitch Size**: 112 × 77 yards
Record Attendance: –	**Ground Capacity**: 25,000

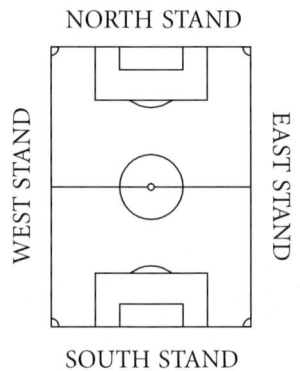

NORTH STAND

WEST STAND   EAST STAND

SOUTH STAND

GENERAL INFORMATION
Supporters Club: Gerry McGreevy, c/o The Club
Telephone Nº: (0118) 968-1100
Car Parking: 1,800 spaces available at the ground
Coach Parking: By Police direction (at the ground)
Nearest Railway Station: Reading Central
Nearest Bus Station: Reading
Club Shop: At the ground
Opening Times: Weekdays and Matchdays 9.00am
to 5.00pm
Telephone Nº: (0118) 968-1234
Postal Sales: Yes
Nearest Police Station: Castle Street, Reading
Police Telephone Nº: (0118) 953-6000

GROUND INFORMATION
Away Supporters' Entrances & Sections:
South Stand entrances and accommodation

ADMISSION INFO (1998/99 PRICES)
Adult Seating: £12.00 – £20.00
Child/Concessions Seating: £7.00 – £8.00
Programme Price: £2.00
Note: Tickets which are purchased in advance are
cheaper than those bought on the day of the game

DISABLED INFORMATION
Wheelchairs: A total of 128 spaces available for
wheelchairs throughout the stadium
Helpers: Yes
Prices: £7.00 for each disabled person + one helper.
£6.00 if ticket is purchased in advance
Disabled Toilets: One available adjacent to stand
Commentaries for approx. 12 people are available
Are Bookings Necessary: Not usually
Contact: (0118) 968-1100

Travelling Supporters' Information:
Routes: The stadium is situated just off Junction 11 of the M4 near Reading.

ROCHDALE FC

Founded: 1907 (**Entered League:** 1921)
Former Names: Rochdale Town FC
Nickname: 'The Dale'
Ground: Spotland Stadium, Rochdale
OL11 5DS
Record Attendance: 24,231 (10/12/49)
Pitch Size: 114 × 76 yards

Colours: Shirts – Blue and White
Shorts – Blue
Telephone Nº: (01706) 644648
Ticket Office: (01706) 644648
Fax Number: (01706) 648466
Ground Capacity: 9,206
Seating Capacity: 4,804

W.M.G. STAND
(Away Seating)

WILLBUTTS LANE
(Away)

MAIN STAND

SANDY LANE END

GENERAL INFORMATION

Supporters Club: F. Duffy, c/o The Club
Telephone Nº: (01706) 852498
Car Parking: W.M.G. Stand car park – £2.00
Coach Parking: By Police direction
Nearest Railway Station: Rochdale (2 miles)
Nearest Bus Station: Town Centre (1 mile)
Club Shop: At Ground
Opening Times: Weekdays 9.15am – 5.15pm and
Matchdays 9.15am – 6.00pm
Telephone Nº: (01706) 647521
Postal Sales: Yes
Nearest Police Station: Rochdale (1½ miles)
Police Telephone Nº: (0161) 872-5050

GROUND INFORMATION

Away Supporters' Entrances & Sections:
Turnstiles 13, 14, 15 and 16 for Willbutts Lane

ADMISSION INFO (1998/99 PRICES)

Adult Standing: £8.00
Adult Seating: £8.00 – £10.00
Child Standing: £4.00 (No concessions in Willbutts
Lane)
Child Seating: £4.00 – £5.00
Additional child concessions are available in the
Family Section of the W.M.G. Stand only.
Programme Price: £1.60

DISABLED INFORMATION

Wheelchairs: 24 spaces in total for Home and Away
fans in the disabled sections, Main & W.M.G. Stands
Helpers: One helper admitted per disabled person
Prices: Free of charge for disabled. Helpers £8.00
Disabled Toilets: Available adjacent to disabled area
Are Bookings Necessary: Yes
Contact: (01706) 644648

Travelling Supporters' Information:
Routes: From All Parts: Exit M62 at Junction 20 following signs for Rochdale. After 1½ miles take the 2nd exit at
the 2nd roundabout into Roch Valley Way signposted Blackburn. At the next traffic lights go straight ahead and
the ground is on the right after ½ mile.

ROTHERHAM UNITED FC

Founded: 1884 (**Entered League:** 1893)
Former Names: Thornhill United FC
(1884-1905); Rotherham County FC
(1905-1925)
Nickname: 'The Merry Millers'
Ground: Millmoor Ground, Rotherham,
S60 1HR
Record Attendance: 25,000 (13/12/52)

Colours: Shirts – Red
       Shorts – White
Telephone Nº: (01709) 512434
Ticket Office: (01709) 512434
Fax Number: (01709) 512762
Pitch Size: 115 × 71 yards
Ground Capacity: 11,533
Seating Capacity: 4,454

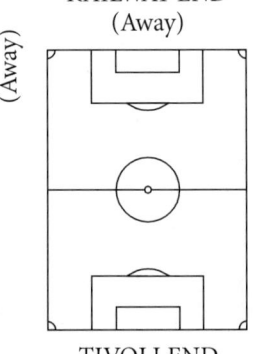

RAILWAY END
(Away)

MILLMOOR LANE STAND (Away)

MAIN STAND

TIVOLI END
MASBOROUGH STREET

GENERAL INFORMATION

Supporters Club: Mrs. Janet Oglesby, c/o Club
Telephone Nº: (0114) 246-3010
Car Parking: Kimberworth Road and Main Street
car parks
Coach Parking: By Police direction
Nearest Railway Station: Rotherham Central (½ m)
Nearest Bus Station: Town Centre (½ mile)
Club Shop: At Ground
Opening Times: Weekdays 9.00am – 5.00pm
Telephone Nº: (01709) 512760
Postal Sales: Yes
Nearest Police Station: Rotherham (½ mile)
Police Telephone Nº: (01709) 371121

GROUND INFORMATION

Away Supporters' Entrances & Sections:
Millmoor Lane turnstiles for Millmoor Lane/
Railway End

ADMISSION INFO (1998/99 PRICES)

Adult Standing: £8.00
Adult Seating: £8.50 – £10.00
Child Standing: £5.00
Child Seating: £5.50 – £6.50
Family Stand: Adults £8.00 + £1.00 for 1st child &
       £5.50 each for others
Programme Price: £1.50

DISABLED INFORMATION

Wheelchairs: 13 spaces in total for Home and Away
fans in the disabled section, Millmoor Lane
Helpers: One helper admitted per disabled person
Prices: Disabled and helpers £5.00 each. Wheelchair
disabled are admitted free of charge
Disabled Toilets: One available in the disabled area
Are Bookings Necessary: Yes
Contact: (01709) 512434

Travelling Supporters' Information:
Routes: From North: Exit M1 at Junction 34 following Rotherham (A6109) signs to traffic lights and turn right.
Ground is ¼ mile on right over railway bridge; From South & West: Exit M1 at Junction 33, turn right following
Rotherham signs. Left at roundabout and right at next roundabout. Follow dual carriageway to next roundabout
and go straight on. Turn left at next roundabout – ground is ¼ mile on left; From East: Take A630 into Rotherham
following Sheffield signs. At 2nd roundabout turn right into Masborough Street then left into Millmoor Lane.

SCARBOROUGH FC

Founded: 1879 (**Entered League**: 1987)	**Colours**: Shirts – White
Former Names: None	Shorts – White
Nickname: 'Boro'	**Telephone Nº**: (01723) 375094
Ground: McCain Stadium, Seamer Road,	**Ticket Office**: (01723) 375094
Scarborough, N. Yorkshire YO12 4HF	**Fax Number**: (01723) 378733
Record Attendance: 11,124 (1938)	**Ground Capacity**: 6,899
Pitch Size: 112 × 74 yards	**Seating Capacity**: 3,500

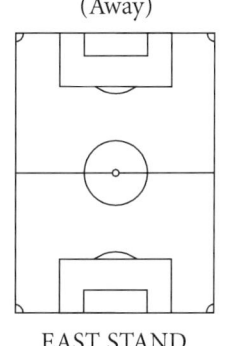

WEST STAND
(Away)

CAR PARK McCAIN STAND

MAIN STAND

EAST STAND
SEAMER ROAD

GENERAL INFORMATION

Supporters Club: Mr. E. Pickup, c/o The Club
Telephone Nº: (01723) 375094
Car Parking: Street Parking
Coach Parking: Scarborough Coach Park
Nearest Railway Station: Scarborough Central
(2 miles)
Nearest Bus Station: Westwood Scarborough
(2 miles)
Club Shop: At Ground
Opening Times: Weekdays 9.30am – 5.00pm and
Matchdays
Telephone Nº: (01723) 375094
Postal Sales: Yes
Nearest Police Station: Scarborough (2 miles)
Police Telephone Nº: (01723) 500300

GROUND INFORMATION

Away Supporters' Entrances & Sections:
West Stand turnstiles for West Stand seating only

ADMISSION INFO (1998/99 PRICES)

Adult Standing: £8.00 (Home End only)
Adult Seating: £10.50
Child Standing: £2.50 (Home End only)
Child Seating: £6.50
Programme Price: £1.50

DISABLED INFORMATION

Wheelchairs: 20 spaces in total in the Main Stand,
West Stand and East Stand
Helpers: One helper admitted per wheelchair
Prices: Full-price for helpers. Free for disabled
Disabled Toilets: Available at rear of disabled area
Are Bookings Necessary: Yes
Contact: (01723) 375094

Travelling Supporters' Information:
Routes: The ground is situated on the main York to Scarborough Road (A64), ½ mile on the left past the B&Q DIY
store.

SCUNTHORPE UNITED FC

Founded: 1899 (**Entered League:** 1950)
Former Names: Scunthorpe and Lindsey United (1899-1912)
Nickname: 'The Iron'
Ground: Glanford Park, Doncaster Road, Scunthorpe, North Lincs.   DN15 8TD
Record Attendance: 8,775 (1/5/89)

Colours: Shirts – White with claret/blue
Shorts – White with claret/blue
Telephone Nº: (01724) 848077
Ticket Office: (01724) 848077
Fax Number: (01724) 857986
Pitch Size: 111 × 73 yards
Ground Capacity: 9,200
Seating Capacity: 6,400

CAPARO MERCHANT BAR STAND (Away)

G.M.B. STAND (Disabled)

SCUNTHORPE EVENING TELEGRAPH STAND

BRITISH STEEL STAND

GENERAL INFORMATION
Supporters Club: None
Telephone Nº: –
Car Parking: Spaces for 600 cars at the ground
Coach Parking: At the ground
Nearest Railway Station: Scunthorpe (1½ miles)
Nearest Bus Station: Scunthorpe (1½ miles)
Club Shop: At the ground
Opening Times: Weekdays 9.00am – 5.00pm
Matchdays 10.30am – 3.00pm & 4.45pm – 5.15pm
Telephone Nº: (01724) 848077
Postal Sales: Yes
Nearest Police Station: Laneham Street, Scunthorpe (1½ miles)
Police Telephone Nº: (01724) 282888

GROUND INFORMATION
Away Supporters' Entrances & Sections:
Turnstiles 6-7 for the Caparo Merchant Bar Stand

ADMISSION INFO (1998/99 PRICES)
Adult Standing: £7.00
Adult Seating: £9.00 – £10.00
Child Standing: £3.50
Child Seating: £4.50 – £5.50
Additional child concessions are available when purchased in advance
Programme Price: £1.70

DISABLED INFORMATION
Wheelchairs: 12 spaces each for Home and Away fans in the disabled section, G.M.B. Stand
Helpers: One helper admitted per disabled person
Prices: Free for the disabled. Helpers full-price
Disabled Toilets: One available in the disabled area
Commentaries are available for the blind
Are Bookings Necessary: Yes
Contact: (01724) 848077

Travelling Supporters' Information:
Routes: From All Parts: Exit M180 at Junction 3 onto M181. Follow M181 to roundabout with A18 and take A18 towards Scunthorpe – the ground is on the right 200 yards from the roundabout.

SHEFFIELD UNITED FC

Founded: 1889 (**Entered League**: 1892)	**Colours**: Shirts – Red and White Stripes
Former Names: None	Shorts – Black
Nickname: 'Blades'	**Telephone Nº**: (0114) 221-5757
Ground: Bramall Lane, Sheffield S2 4SU	**Ticket Office**: (0114) 221-1889
Record Attendance: 68,287 (15/2/36)	**Fax Number**: (0114) 272-3030
	Pitch Size: 112 × 72 yards
	Ground Capacity: 30,376 (All seats)

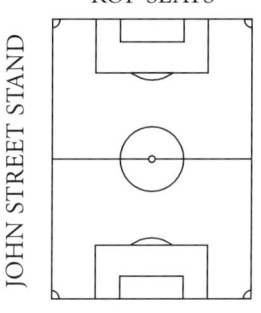

SHOREHAM STREET
KOP SEATS

JOHN STREET STAND

CHERRY STREET
LAVER STAND

LOWER (Away)
UPPER (Home)
WARDS BREWERY
STAND

GENERAL INFORMATION

Supporters Club: c/o Beryl Whitney, 42 Base Green Avenue, Sheffield S12 3FA
Telephone Nº: (0114) 239-0202
Car Parking: Street Parking
Coach Parking: By Police direction
Nearest Railway Station: Sheffield Midland (1 mile)
Nearest Bus Station: Pond Street, Sheffield
Club Shop: At Ground
Opening Times: Monday to Friday 9.30am – 5.00pm & Matchdays 9.30am – 5.30pm
Telephone Nº: (0114) 221-3129
Postal Sales: Yes
Nearest Police Station: Police Room at the ground
Police Telephone Nº: (0114) 276-8522

GROUND INFORMATION

Away Supporters' Entrances & Sections:
Bramall Lane turnstiles – Bramall Lane Lower Stand

ADMISSION INFO (1998/99 PRICES)

Adult Seating: £11.00 – £17.00
Child Seating: £4.00 – £9.00
Programme Price: £1.80

DISABLED INFORMATION

Wheelchairs: Limited number of spaces available in the disabled section – Members area
Helpers: One helper admitted per wheelchair
Prices: Contact the club for further details
Disabled Toilets: 3 available within the enclosure
Commentaries available for the blind on request
Are Bookings Necessary: Yes
Contact: (0114) 221-5757

Travelling Supporters' Information:
Routes: From North: Exit M1 at Junction 34 following signs to Sheffield (A6109), turn left after 3½ miles and take 4th exit at the roundabout into Sheaf Street. Take the 5th exit at the 2nd roundabout into St. Mary's Road (for Bakewell), turn left ½ mile into Bramall Lane; From South and East: Exit M1 at Junctions 31 or 33 and take A57 to the roundabout, take the 3rd exit into Sheaf Street (then as North); From West: Take A57 into Sheffield and take 4th exit at roundabout into Upper Hanover Street, at 2nd roundabout take 3rd exit into Bramall Lane.

SHEFFIELD WEDNESDAY FC

Founded: 1867 (**Entered League**: 1892)
Former Names: The Wednesday FC
Nickname: 'Owls'
Ground: Hillsborough, Sheffield S6 1SW
Record Attendance: 72,841 (17/2/34)

Colours: Shirts – Blue and White Stripes
Shorts – Black
Telephone Nº: (0114) 221-2121
Ticket Office: (0114) 221-2400
Fax Number: (0114) 221-2122
Pitch Size: 115 × 74 yards
Ground Capacity: 39,814 (All seats)

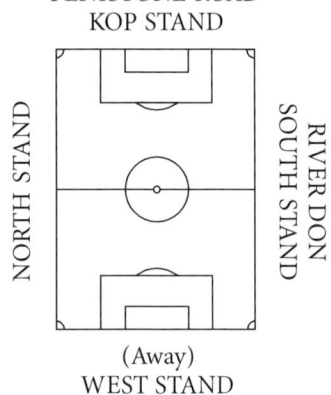

PENISTONE ROAD
KOP STAND

NORTH STAND

RIVER DON
SOUTH STAND

(Away)
WEST STAND

GENERAL INFORMATION

Supporters Club: –
Telephone Nº: –
Car Parking: Street Parking
Coach Parking: Owlerton Stadium
Nearest Railway Station: Sheffield Midland (4 mls)
Nearest Bus Station: Pond Street, Sheffield (4 miles)
Club Shop: At Ground & Orchard Square
Ground Opening Times: Monday to Saturday
9.00am – 5.00pm
Telelphone Nº: (0114) 221-2345
Orchard Square Opening Times: Monday to
Saturday 9.00am – 5.30pm
Telephone Nº: (0114) 221-2350
Postal Sales: Yes – via the Club Shop
Nearest Police Station: Hammerton Road, Sheffield
(1 mile)
Police Telephone Nº: (0114) 276-8522

GROUND INFORMATION

Away Supporters' Entrances & Sections:
West Stand turnstiles for West Stand, Upper Tier

ADMISSION INFO (1998/99 PRICES)

Adult Seating: £13.00 – £24.00
Child Seating: £7.00 – £15.00
Programme Price: £2.00
Note: Prices vary depending on category of game

DISABLED INFORMATION

Wheelchairs: Unspecified number of spaces in the
disabled section – North Stand & West Stand Lower
Helpers: One helper admitted per disabled person
Prices: No charge for the disabled and helpers
Disabled Toilets: Available within the North Stand
Commentaries are available for the blind
Are Bookings Necessary: Yes
Contact: (0114) 221-2121

Travelling Supporters' Information:
Routes: From North: Exit M1 at Junction 34 following signs for Sheffield (A6109), after 1½ miles take the 3rd
exit at the roundabout and after 3¼ miles turn left into Herries Road for the ground; From South and East: Exit
M1 at Junctions 31 or 33 and take A57 to the roundabout and take the exit into Prince of Wales Road. After 5¾
miles turn left into Herries Road South; From West: Take A57 until A6101 and turn left. After 3¾ miles turn left
at the 'T' junction into Penistone Road for the ground.

SHREWSBURY TOWN FC

Founded: 1886 **(Entered League:** 1950)
Former Names: None
Nickname: 'Town'
Ground: Gay Meadow, Shrewsbury, SY2 6AB
Record Attendance: 18,917 (26/4/61)
Pitch Size: 116 × 75 yards

Colours: Shirts – Blue with White Trim
Shorts – Blue with White Trim
Telephone Nº: (01743) 360111
Ticket Office: (01743) 360111
Fax Number: (01743) 236384
Ground Capacity: 8,000
Seating Capacity: 3,000

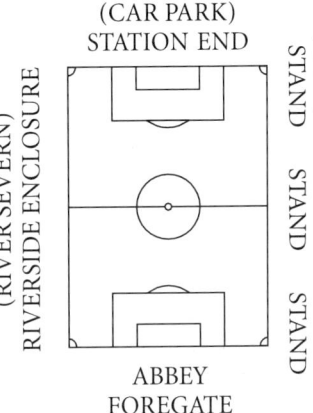

(CAR PARK)
STATION END

(RIVER SEVERN) RIVERSIDE ENCLOSURE

STATION STAND — STATION CENTRE STAND — CENTRE WAKEMAN STAND

ABBEY FOREGATE

GENERAL INFORMATION

Supporters Club: Alan Follmer, c/o The Club
Telephone Nº: (01743) 360111
Car Parking: Car park adjacent to the ground
Coach Parking: Gay Meadow
Nearest Railway Station: Shrewsbury (1 mile)
Nearest Bus Station: Raven Meadows, Shrewsbury
Club Shop: At Ground
Opening Times: Matchdays and Office Hours
Telephone Nº: (01743) 356316
Postal Sales: Yes
Nearest Police Station: Clive Road, Shrewsbury
Police Telephone Nº: (01743) 232888

GROUND INFORMATION

Away Supporters' Entrances & Sections:
Station End turnstiles for Station Stand (covered)

ADMISSION INFO (1998/99 PRICES)

Adult Standing: £8.00
Adult Seating: £10.00 – £12.00 (Members only)
Child Standing: £5.00 (Members only)
Child Seating: £6.00 (Wakeman Stand)
Away Standing: £8.00 (Concessions £5.00)
Away Seating: £10.00 (Concessions £7.00)
Programme Price: £1.50

DISABLED INFORMATION

Wheelchairs: 4 spaces each for home fans and away fans in two areas at the side of the stands
Helpers: One helper admitted per disabled person
Prices: Free for the disabled. £5.00 for helpers
Disabled Toilets: One available in Wakeman Stand
Are Bookings Necessary: Yes
Contact: (01743) 356316

Travelling Supporters' Information:
Routes: From North: Take A49 or A53 then 2nd exit at the roundabout into Telford Way (A5112). After ¾ mile take 2nd exit at the roundabout. Turn right at 'T' junction into Abbey Foregate for the ground; From South: Take A49 to the Town Centre and at the end of Coleham Head turn right into Abbey Foregate; From East: Take A5 then A458 into the Town Centre and go straight forward into Abbey Foregate; From West: Take A458 then A5 around Ring Road to Roman Road, then turn left into Hereford Road and at the end of Coleman Head turn right into Abbey Foregate.

SOUTHAMPTON FC

Founded: 1885 (**Entered League:** 1920)
Former Names: Southampton St. Mary's
YMCA FC (1885-1897)
Nickname: 'Saints'
Ground: The Dell, Milton Road,
Southampton SO15 2XH
Record Attendance: 31,044 (8/10/69)

Colours: Shirts – Red and White
Shorts – Black
Telephone Nº: (01703) 220505
Ticket Office: (01703) 220505
Fax Number: (01703) 330360
Pitch Size: 110×72 yards
Ground Capacity: 15,000 (All seats)

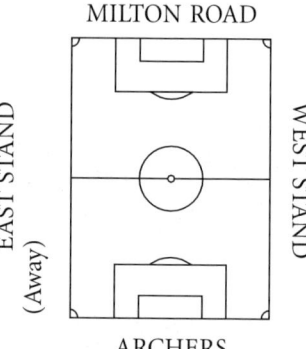

WILTON AVENUE
MILTON ROAD

EAST STAND
(Away)

HILL LANE/MILTON ROAD
WEST STAND

ARCHERS
ROAD END

GENERAL INFORMATION

Supporters Club: c/o The Secretary, Saints Supporters' Social Club, The Dell, Milton Road, Southampton
Telephone Nº: (01703) 336540
Car Parking: Street Parking
Coach Parking: By Police direction
Nearest Railway Stat'n: Southampton Central (1ml)
Nearest Bus Station: West Quay Road by Centre 2000
Club Shop: At Ground
Opening Times: Monday to Saturday 9.00am – 5.00pm (closed Wednesday)
Telephone Nº: (01703) 236400
Postal Sales: Yes
Nearest Police Station: Civic Centre, Southampton (1 mile)
Police Telephone Nº: (01703) 335444

GROUND INFORMATION

Away Supporters' Entrances & Sections:
Archers Road turnstiles 16-20 for Upper/Lower East Stand Archers Road End

ADMISSION INFO (1998/99 PRICES)
Adult Seating: £18.00 – £20.00
Child Seating: £8.00
Note: There are no concessions for away fans
Programme Price: £2.00

DISABLED INFORMATION
Wheelchairs: 18 spaces in total for Home and Away fans in the disabled section, under the West Stand
Helpers: One helper admitted per disabled person
Prices: Free of charge for disabled. Helpers £15.00
Disabled Toilets: Available by the disabled entrance
Commentaries are available for the blind
Are Bookings Necessary: Yes
Contact: (01703) 667547 (Mr. Mortimer)

Travelling Supporters' Information:
Routes: From North: Take A33 into the Avenue and turn right into Northlands Road. Turn right at the end into Archer's Road; From East: Take M27 to A334 and follow signs Southampton A3024. Follow signs for The West into Commercial Road, turn right into Hill Lane then 1st right into Milton Road; From West: Take A35 then A3024 following signs for City Centre into Fourposts Hill then left into Hill Lane and 1st right into Milton Road.

SOUTHEND UNITED FC

Founded: 1906 (**Entered League:** 1920)	**Colours:** Shirts – Blue with white/black/grey
Former Names: Southend Athletic FC	Shorts – Blue
Nickname: 'Shrimpers'; 'Blues'	**Telephone N°:** (01702) 304050
Ground: Roots Hall Ground, Victoria Avenue, Southend-on-Sea SS2 6NQ	**Ticket Office:** (01702) 304090
Record Attendance: 31,033 (10/1/79)	**Fax Number:** (01702) 330164
Pitch Size: 110 × 74 yards	**Ground Capacity:** 12,306 (All seats)

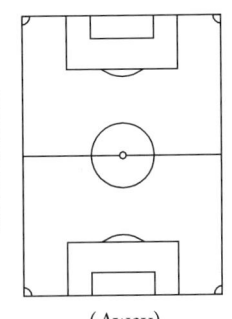

SOUTH BANK

VICTORIA AVENUE
EAST STAND

SHAKESPEARE DRIVE
WEST STAND

(Away)
NORTH STAND
FAIRFAX DRIVE

GENERAL INFORMATION

Supporters Club: Mr. T. Hall, c/o 9 Ness Road, Shoeburyness, Essex SS3 9DE
Telephone N°: (01702) 304050
Car Parking: Car park at the ground for 500 cars – Season Ticket holders only + Street parking
Coach Parking: Car park at the ground
Nearest Railway Station: Prittlewell (¼ mile)
Nearest Bus Station: London Road, Southend
Club Shop: At the ground and in Town
Opening Times: Ground: Matchdays only
Town Shop: Monday to Saturday 9.30am – 5.00pm
Telephone N°: (01702) 304140 (Ground);
(01702) 601351 (Town Shop)
Postal Sales: Yes
Nearest Police Station: Southend-on-Sea (¼ mile)
Police Telephone N°: (01702) 431212

GROUND INFORMATION

Away Supporters' Entrances & Sections:
North Stand turnstiles for North Stand seating

ADMISSION INFO (1998/99 PRICES)

Adult Seating: £8.00 – £12.00
Child Seating: £4.00 – £5.00
Away Seating: £10.00 (purchased on matchday – concessions available on a reciprocal basis)
Programme Price: £1.60

DISABLED INFORMATION

Wheelchairs: 20 spaces in total for Home and Away fans in the disabled section, West Stand
Helpers: One helper admitted per disabled person
Prices: £5.00 per wheelchair. £10.00 per adult helper. £5.00 per concessionary helper
Disabled Toilets: One available in the disabled area
Commentaries are available for the blind
Are Bookings Necessary: Yes
Contact: (01702) 304090

Travelling Supporters' Information:
Routes: From North and West: From the M25 take Junction 19 and follow the A127 to Southend. About 1 mile outside of Southend Town Centre, take the 3rd exit at the roundabout into Victoria Avenue for the ground; From the A13: Following signs for Southend, turn left into West Road at Westcliff. At the end of West Road turn left into Victoria Avenue and the ground is on the left.

STOCKPORT COUNTY FC

Founded: 1883 (**Entered League:** 1900)
Former Names: Heaton Norris Rovers FC and Heaton Norris FC
Nickname: 'Hatters' 'County'
Ground: Edgeley Park, Hardcastle Road, Edgeley, Stockport SK3 9DD
Record Attendance: 27,833 (11/2/50)

Colours: Shirts – Blue and White Stripes
Shorts – Blue with White Trim
Telephone Nº: (0161) 286-8888
Ticket Office: (0161) 286-8888
Fax Number: (0161) 286-8900
Pitch Size: 111 × 72 yards
Ground Capacity: 9,491

RAILWAY END
(Away)

HARDCASTLE ROAD STAND

VERNON BUILDING SOCIETY STAND

CHEADLE STAND

GENERAL INFORMATION

Supporters Club: Des Hinks, Independent Supporters' Club
Telephone Nº: (0161) 476-6703
Car Parking: Street Parking
Coach Parking: By Police direction
Nearest Railway Station: Stockport (5 mins. walk)
Nearest Bus Station: Mersey Square (10 mins. walk)
Club Shop: At Ground
Opening Times: Weekdays 9.30am – 5.30pm and Saturdays 9.30am – 1.00pm
Telephone Nº: (0161) 286-8899
Postal Sales: Yes
Nearest Police Station: Stockport (1 mile)
Police Telephone Nº: (0161) 872-5050

GROUND INFORMATION

Away Supporters' Entrances & Sections:
Railway End turnstiles for Railway End

ADMISSION INFO (1998/99 PRICES)

Adult Seating: £13.00 – £15.00
Child Seating: £6.00 for one child. More than one child – £3.00 each
OAP Seating: £8.00
Away Fans: £13.00 (away concessions offered on a reciprocal basis only)
Programme Price: £1.80

DISABLED INFORMATION

Wheelchairs: 16 spaces in total. 10 in the Hardcastle Road Stand, 6 in the Cheadle Stand
Helpers: One helper admitted per disabled fan
Prices: Free for the disabled. Helpers full-price
Disabled Toilets: Yes
Are Bookings Necessary: Yes
Contact: (0161) 286-8888

Travelling Supporters' Information:
Routes: From North, South and West: Exit M63 at Junction 11 and join A560, following signs for Cheadle, after ¼ mile turn right into Edgeley Road and after 1 mile turn right into Caroline Street for the ground; From East: Take A6 or A560 into Stockport Town Centre and turn left into Greek Street. Take 2nd exit into Mercian Way (from roundabout) then turn left into Caroline Street – the ground is straight ahead.

STOKE CITY FC

Founded: 1863 (**Entered League**: 1888)
Former Names: Stoke FC
Nickname: 'Potters'
Ground: Britannia Stadium, Stanley Matthews Way, Stoke-on-Trent ST4 4EG
Record Attendance: —
Pitch Size: 115 × 75 yards

Colours: Shirts – Red and White Stripes
Shorts – White
Telephone Nº: (01782) 592222
Ticket Office: (01782) 592200
Fax Number: (01782) 592221
Ground Capacity: 28,000

NORTH STAND

McEWANS STAND

SENTINEL STAND

(Away)
SIGNAL RADIO STAND

GENERAL INFORMATION

Supporters Club: c/o Nic Mansfield, 11A Westland Street, Penkhull, Stoke-on-Trent   ST4 7HE
Telephone Nº: (01782) 744674
Car Parking: At the ground (bookings necessary). Also various car parks within 10 minutes walk
Coach Parking: At the ground
Nearest Railway Station: Stoke-on-Trent (1½ miles)
Nearest Bus Station: Glebe Street, Stoke-on-Trent
Club Shop: At the ground
Opening Times: Monday to Friday 9.00am – 5.30pm & non-match Saturdays 9.30am – 12.00pm. Saturday Matchdays 9.00am to kick-off and Final whistle to 5.30pm. Evening matchdays 5.30pm to kick-off and Final whistle to 10.00pm
Telephone Nº: (01782) 592244
Postal Sales: Yes
Nearest Police Station: Stoke-on-Trent (1 mile)
Police Telephone Nº: (01782) 744644

GROUND INFORMATION

Away Supporters' Entrances & Sections:
Signal Radio South Stand

ADMISSION INFO (1998/99 PRICES)

Adult Seating: £11.00 – £16.00
Child Seating: £7.00 – £9.00 (less in Family Area)
Note: No cash accepted at the turnstiles – tickets can be purchased from the ticket office
Programme Price: £1.80

DISABLED INFORMATION

Wheelchairs: 164 spaces available in total
Helpers: One helper admitted per disabled person
Prices: £5.00 for the disabled. Adult helpers normal prices, Concessionary helpers concessionary prices
Disabled Toilets: Yes
Commentaries are available – phone for details
Are Bookings Necessary: Yes
Contact: (01782) 592200

Travelling Supporters' Information:
Routes: From the North, South and West: Exit M6 at Junction 15 and take the A500 to Stoke-on-Trent. At the first exit, take the A34 to Stone and follow signs for Trentham. At the next roundabout, turn left onto Trentham Road (A5035) and carry on until you reach the traffic signalised junction which sits on the southern entrance to Stanley Matthews Way; From the East: Take the A50 to Stoke-on-Trent and leave at the Longton Exit into Trentham Road (A5035). Stay on Trentham Road until you reach the traffic signalised junction which sits on the southern entrance to Stanley Matthews Way.

SUNDERLAND FC

Founded: 1879 (**Entered League:** 1890)
Former Names: Sunderland and District
Teachers FC
Nickname: 'Rokerites'
Ground: Stadium of Light, Sunderland,
SR5 1SU
Record Attendance: —

Colours: Shirts – Red and White Stripes
Shorts – Black
Telephone N°: (0191) 551-5000
Ticket Office: (0191) 551-5151
Fax Number: (0191) 551-5123
Pitch Size: 115 × 75 yards
Ground Capacity: 41,590 (All seats)

Photo courtesy of Sunderland AFC

METRO FM STAND
(Away)

McEWAN STAND

WEST STAND
McDONALDs FAMILY
ENCLOSURE

NORTH STAND

GENERAL INFORMATION

Supporters Club: c/o Audrey Baillie, 1/2 Monk
Street, Monkwearmouth, Sunderland SR5 0DB
Telephone N°: (0191) 567-0067
Car Parking: Spaces for 1,100 cars (reserved)
Coach Parking: At the ground
Nearest Railway Station: Sunderland (1 mile)
Nearest Bus Station: Town Centre (1 mile)
Club Shop: Town Centre
Opening Times: Monday to Saturday 9.00am –
5.00pm
Telephone N°: (0191) 551-5050
Postal Sales: Yes
Nearest Police Station: Southwick (½ mile)
Police Telephone N°: (0191) 510-2020

GROUND INFORMATION

Away Supporters' Entrances & Sections:
Metro FM Stand

ADMISSION INFO (1998/99 PRICES)

Adult Seating: £12.00 – £21.00
Child Seating: Not known at time of publication
Programme Price: £1.50

DISABLED INFORMATION

Wheelchairs: Detailed information was unavailable
at the time of publication.
Helpers: –
Prices: –
Disabled Toilets: Yes
Are Bookings Necessary: Yes
Contact: (0191) 551-5000

Travelling Supporters' Information:
Routes: From All Parts: Exit A1 at A690 Durham/Sunderland exit. After approximately 4 miles turn left onto
A19 (signposted Tyne Tunnel). Keep in the left lane and take the slip road (signposted Washington/Sunderland)
onto the bridge over the River Wear. Turn right onto A1231 (signposted Washington/Sunderland), stay on this
road going straight across 4 roundabouts into Sunderland. Continue straight through 2 sets of traffic lights and
the Stadium car park is on the right, about 1 mile past the traffic lights.

SWANSEA CITY FC

<table>
<tr><td>

Founded: 1900 (**Entered League**: 1920)
Former Names: Swansea Town FC (1900-1970)
Nickname: 'Swans'
Ground: Vetch Field, Swansea SA1 3SU
Record Attendance: 32,796 (17/2/68)
Pitch Size: 110 × 74 yards

</td><td>

Colours: Shirts – White with black & maroon
        Shorts – White with black & maroon
Telephone Nº: (01792) 474114
Ticket Office: (01792) 462584
Fax Number: (01792) 646120
Ground Capacity: 9,975
Seating Capacity: 3,414

</td></tr>
</table>

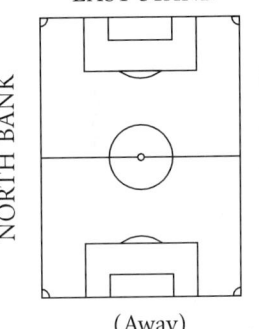

WILLIAM STREET
EAST STAND

MADOC STREET / NORTH BANK

GLAMORGAN STREET / CENTRE STAND

(Away)
WEST TERRACE
RICHARDSON STREET

GENERAL INFORMATION

Supporters Club: c/o Club
Telephone Nº: (01792) 474114
Car Parking: Kingsway (200 yards) and Clarence Terrace (50 yards) Car Parks + street parking
Coach Parking: By Police direction
Nearest Railway Station: Swansea High Street (1ml)
Nearest Bus Station: Quadrant Depot (¼ mile)
Club Shop: 33 William Street, Swansea SA1 3QS
Opening Times: Weekdays 10.00am – 4.30pm and Matchdays 9.30am – 5.00pm
Telephone Nº: (01792) 462584
Postal Sales: Yes
Nearest Police Station: Swansea Central (1 mile)
Police Telephone Nº: (01792) 456999

GROUND INFORMATION

Away Supporters' Entrances & Sections:
Richardson Street turnstiles for the West Terrace Enclosure (partially covered)

ADMISSION INFO (1998/99 PRICES)

Adult Standing: £8.00
Adult Seating: £11.00 – £12.00
Child Standing: £4.00
Child Seating: Adult + 1 child = £15.00   Adult + 2 children = £17.00
Programme Price: £1.70

DISABLED INFORMATION

Wheelchairs: 10 spaces in total for Home and Away fans in the disabled section, Centre Stand touchline
Helpers: One helper admitted per wheelchair
Prices: £4.00 for disabled fan and 1 helper
Disabled Toilets: None
Are Bookings Necessary: Yes
Contact: (01792) 474114

Travelling Supporters' Information:
Routes: From All Parts: Exit M4 at Junction 42 and follow Swansea (A483) signs. After 4 miles follow signs for City Centre West. After ½ turn right (opposite County Hall) into West Way. At first set of traffic lights, turn left into Glamorgan Street from Vetch Field.

SWINDON TOWN FC

Founded: 1881 (**Entered League:** 1920)
Former Names: None
Nickname: 'Robins'
Ground: County Ground, County Road, Swindon SN1 2ED
Record Attendance: 32,000 (15/1/72)
Pitch Size: 114 × 74 yards

Colours: Shirts – Red
Shorts – Red
Telephone Nº: (01793) 430430
Ticket Office: (01793) 529000
Fax Number: (01793) 536170
Ground Capacity: 15,728 (All seats)

ROVER FAMILY STAND

SOUTH STAND

ARKELL'S STAND

(Away)
STRATTON
BANK

GENERAL INFORMATION

Supporters Club: c/o Mr. Dave Cummings, 10 Cadley Close, Swindon, Wilts SN2 1SP
Telephone Nº: (01793) 539998
Car Parking: Town Centre
Coach Parking: Car park adjacent to the ground
Nearest Railway Station: Swindon (½ mile)
Nearest Bus Station: Swindon (½ mile)
Club Shop: The Swindon Town Superstore
Opening Times: Weekdays 8.30am – 5.45pm and Saturdays 10.00am – 4.00pm. Matchdays 9.00am to 3.00pm
Telephone Nº: (01793) 423030
Postal Sales: Yes
Nearest Police Station: Fleming Way, Swindon
Police Telephone Nº: (01793) 528111

GROUND INFORMATION

Away Supporters' Entrances & Sections:
Arkell's Stand turnstiles for the Stratton Bank

ADMISSION INFO (1998/99 PRICES)

Adult Seating: £14.00 – £17.50
Child Seating: Free (aged 15 and under)
Programme Price: £2.00

DISABLED INFORMATION

Wheelchairs: 56 spaces in total for Home and Away fans in the disabled section, Rover Family Stand
Helpers: One helper admitted per disabled person
Prices: £5.50 for 1 wheelchair + 1 helper
Disabled Toilets: Available within the disabled area
Commentaries are available for the blind
Are Bookings Necessary: Yes
Contact: (01793) 529000

Travelling Supporters' Information:
Routes: From London, East and South: Exit M4 at Junction 15 and take A345 into Swindon along Queen's Drive. Take the 3rd exit at 'Magic Roundabout' into County Road; From West: Exit M4 at Junction 15 then as above; From North: Take M4 or A345/A420/A361 to County Road roundabout, then as above.

TORQUAY UNITED FC

Founded: 1899 (**Entered League:** 1927)	**Colours:** Shirts – Yellow and Navy Stripes
Former Names: Torquay Town (**1899-1910**)	Shorts – Navy
Nickname: 'Gulls'	**Telephone Nº:** (01803) 328666
Ground: Plainmoor Ground, Torquay,	**Ticket Office:** (01803) 328666
TQ1 3PS	**Fax Number:** (01803) 323976
Record Attendance: 21,908 (29/1/55)	**Ground Capacity:** 6,003
Pitch Size: 110 × 74 yards	**Seating Capacity:** 2,446

ELLACOMBE END

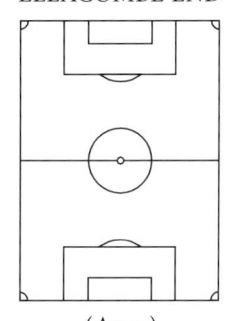

HOMELANDS LANE GRAND STAND

MARNHAM ROAD POPULAR SIDE

(Away)
BABBACOMBE END
WARBRO ROAD

GENERAL INFORMATION

Supporters Club: None
Telephone Nº: –
Car Parking: Street Parking
Coach Parking: Lymington Road Coach Station (½ mile)
Nearest Railway Station: Torquay (2 miles)
Nearest Bus Station: Lymington Road (½ mile)
Club Shop: At Ground
Opening Times: Matchdays & during Office Hours
Telephone Nº: (01803) 328666
Postal Sales: Yes
Nearest Police Station: Torquay (1 mile)
Police Telephone Nº: (0990) 777444

GROUND INFORMATION

Away Supporters' Entrances & Sections:
Babbacombe End turnstiles for Babbacombe End

ADMISSION INFO (1998/99 PRICES)

Adult Standing: £8.00
Adult Seating: £9.00
Concessionary Standing: £5.00 (Under-16s £4.00)
Concessionary Seating: £4.00 – £6.00
Note: Under 5's admitted free with an adult
Programme Price: £1.50

DISABLED INFORMATION

Wheelchairs: 30 spaces in total in the disabled section, in front of Ellacombe End Stand
Helpers: One helper admitted per disabled person
Prices: Free of charge for Disabled and Helpers
Disabled Toilets: 2 available within the Main Stand
Audio facilities available for the blind
Are Bookings Necessary: No
Contact: (01803) 328666

Travelling Supporters' Information:
Routes: From North and East: Take M5 to A38 and A380 to Torquay. On entering Torquay, turn left at the 3rd set of traffic lights into Hele Road. Continue straight on over two mini-roundabouts and up West Hill Road to traffic lights, then go straight ahead into Warbro Road. The ground is situated 200 yards on the right.

TOTTENHAM HOTSPUR FC

Founded: 1882 (**Entered League:** 1908)
Former Names: Hotspur FC (1882-1885)
Nickname: 'Spurs'
Ground: White Hart Lane, 748 High Road, Tottenham, London   N17 0AP
Record Attendance: 75,038 (5/3/38)
Pitch Size: 110 × 73 yards

Colours: Shirts – White
             Shorts – Navy Blue
Telephone Nº: (0181) 365-5000
Ticket Office: (0181) 365-5050
Fax Number: (0181) 365-5005
Ground Capacity: 33,147 (All seats)

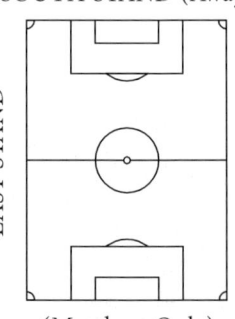

PARK LANE
SOUTH STAND (Away)

WORCESTER AVENUE
EAST STAND

HIGH ROAD
WEST STAND

(Members Only)
NORTH STAND
PAXTON ROAD

GENERAL INFORMATION

Supporters Club: c/o Linda Watkins, Spurs Members Club, 752B High Road, Tottenham N17
Telephone Nº: (0181) 365-5150
Car Parking: None within ¼ mile
Coach Parking: Northumberland Park Coach Park, Leeside Road
Nearest Railway Station: White Hart Lane (Nearby)/Northumberland Park
Nearest Tube Station: Seven Sisters (Victoria); Manor House (Piccadilly)
Club Shop: At Ground
Opening Times: Weekdays 9.30am – 5.30pm and Matchdays 9.30am – 6.00pm
Telephone Nº: (0181) 365-5042
Postal Sales: Yes – Phone (0181) 808-5959
Nearest Police Station: Tottenham (1 mile)
Police Telephone Nº: (0181) 801-3443

GROUND INFORMATION

Away Supporters' Entrances & Sections:
Park Lane entrances for South Stand

ADMISSION INFO (1998/99 PRICES)

Adult Seating: £18.00 – £35.00
Child Seating: £9.00 – £11.00
Note: Additional discounts available for members
Programme Price: £1.80

DISABLED INFORMATION

Wheelchairs: 27 spaces for home fans, 17 for away fans in the disabled areas. Home support: North Stand Lower Tier; Away Support: South Stand
Helpers: One helper admitted per disabled person
Prices: Price for one disabled person + a helper – £18.00
Disabled Toilets: 2 available in Paxton Road Enclosure, 1 near Park Lane
Are Bookings Necessary: Yes
Contact: (0181) 365-5050

Travelling Supporters' Information:
Routes: From All Parts: Take A406 North Circular to Edmonton and at traffic lights follow signs for Tottenham (A1010) into Fore Street for the ground.

TRANMERE ROVERS FC

Founded: 1881 (**Entered League**: 1921)
Former Names: Belmont FC
Nickname: 'Rovers'
Ground: Prenton Park, Prenton Road West, Birkenhead   L42 9PN
Record Attendance: 24,424 (5/2/72)
Pitch Size: 110 × 70 yards

Colours: Shirts – White
              Shorts – Blue
Telephone Nº: (0151) 608-0371/608-4194
Ticket Office: (0151) 609-0137
Fax Number: (0151) 608-4385
Ground Capacity: 16,800 (All seats)

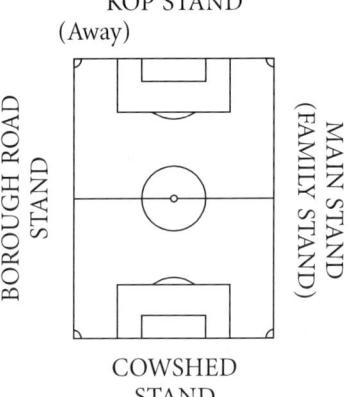

KOP STAND
(Away)

BOROUGH ROAD STAND

MAIN STAND
(FAMILY STAND)

COWSHED STAND

GENERAL INFORMATION

Supporters Club: C. Dalziel, c/o The Club
Telephone Nº: (0151) 608-3677/608-4194
Car Parking: Large car park at ground (£3.00)
Coach Parking: At the ground (£10.00 charge)
Nearest Railway Station: Hamilton Square, Rock Ferry (1 mile)
Nearest Bus Station: Birkenhead
Club Shop: At Ground
Opening Times: Weekdays and Matchdays 9.00am – 5.00pm
Telephone Nº: (0151) 608-0371/608-4194
Postal Sales: Yes
Nearest Police Stat'n: Bebington (2 miles)
Police Telephone Nº: (0151) 709-6010

GROUND INFORMATION

Away Supporters' Entrances & Sections:
Kop Stand turnstiles 22-27 – access from Car Park

ADMISSION INFO (1998/99 PRICES)

Adult Seating: £10.00   £14.00
Child Seating: £5.00 – £7.00
Programme Price: £1.80
Note: Concessionary admission available by prepaid vouchers

DISABLED INFORMATION

Wheelchairs: 28 spaces in total for Home and Away fans in the disabled section, Paddock – Family Stand
Helpers: One helper admitted per disabled person
Prices: Free of charge for disabled. Helpers £11.00
Disabled Toilets: 2 available in the disabled section
Are Bookings Necessary: Yes
Contact: (0151) 609-0137

Travelling Supporters' Information:
Routes: From North: Take Mersey Tunnel to M53, exit Junction 3 and take the 1st exit at the rounabout (A552), after 1¼ miles turn right at crossroads (B5151) then left into Prenton Road West; From South and East: Exit M53 at Junction 4 and take 4th exit at roundabout (B5151). After 2½ miles turn right into Prenton Road West.

WALSALL FC

Founded: 1888 (**Entered League:** 1892)
Former Names: Walsall Town Swifts FC
(1888-1895)
Nickname: 'Saddlers'
Ground: Bescot Stadium, Bescot Crescent
Walsall, West Midlands   WS1 4SA
Record Attendance: 10,628 (2/5/91)

Colours: Shirts – Red with Black Trim
           Shorts – Red with Black Trim
Telephone Nº: (01922) 622791
Ticket Office: (01922) 651410
Fax Number: (01922) 613202
Pitch Size: 110 × 73 yards
Ground Capacity: 9,000
Seating Capacity: 6,685

(BESCOT CRESCENT)
WILLIAM SHARP STAND
(Away)

BANKS'S STAND

H.L. FELLOWS STAND

GILBERT ALSO
STAND

GENERAL INFORMATION
Supporters Club: Saddlers Club
Telephone Nº: (01922) 622257
Car Parking: Car park at the ground
Coach Parking: At the ground
Nearest Railway Station: Bescot (adjacent)
Nearest Bus Station: Bradford Place, Walsall
Club Shop: At Ground and Bradford Street, Walsall
Opening Times: Weekdays and Matchdays 9.00am
– 5.30pm
Telephone Nº: (01922) 613356 (Bradford Street)
Postal Sales: Yes
Nearest Police Station: Walsall (2 miles)
Police Telephone Nº: (01922) 638111

GROUND INFORMATION
Away Supporters' Entrances & Sections:
Turnstiles 21-28 for William Sharp Stand

ADMISSION INFO (1998/99 PRICES)
Adult Standing: £9.00
Adult Seating: £13.00
Child Standing: £7.00
Child Seating: £9.00
Family Ticket: 1 adult + 1 child – £12.00
Programme Price: £1.80

DISABLED INFORMATION
Wheelchairs: 30 spaces in total for Home and Away
fans in the disabled section, Banks's Stand
Helpers: One helper admitted per disabled person
Prices: Free of charge for wheelchair disabled and
one helper each
Disabled Toilets: Adjacent to disabled viewing bays
Are Bookings Necessary: Yes
Contact: (01922) 622791

Travelling Supporters' Information:
Routes: From All Parts: Exit M6 at Junction 9 turning North towards Walsall onto the A461. After ¼ mile turn
right into Wallows Lane and pass over the railway bridge. Then tale 1st right into Bescot Crescent and the ground is
½ mile along on the left adjacent to Bescot Railway Station.

WATFORD FC

Founded: 1891 (**Entered League**: 1920) **Former Names**: Formed by amalgamation of West Herts FC and St. Mary's FC **Nickname**: 'Hornets' **Ground**: Vicarage Road Stadium, Watford WD1 8ER **Record Attendance**: 34,099 (3/2/69)	**Colours**: Shirts – Yellow and Red Shorts – Red **Telephone Nº**: (01923) 496000 **Ticket Office**: (01923) 496000 **Fax Number**: (01923) 496001 **Pitch Size**: 115 × 75 yards **Ground Capacity**: 22,000 (All seats)

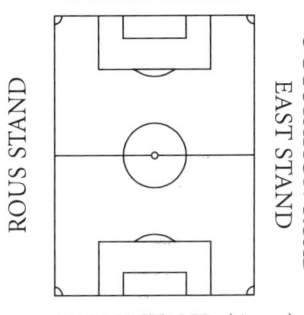

VICARAGE ROAD
NORTH STAND

ROUS STAND

OCCUPATION ROAD EAST STAND

ROOKERY STAND (Away)

GENERAL INFORMATION

Supporters Club: c/o Marketing Department, c/o The Club
Telephone Nº: (01923) 496006
Car Parking: Nearby multi-storey car park
Coach Parking: Cardiff Road car park
Nearest Railway Station: Station at ground (Big Games only) or Watford Junction
Nearest Bus Station: Watford
Club Shop: At Ground
Opening Times: Monday to Saturday 9.00 – 5.00
Telephone Nº: (01923) 496005
Postal Sales: Yes
Nearest Police Station: Shady Lane, Clarendon Road, Watford (1½ miles)
Police Telephone Nº: (01923) 472000

GROUND INFORMATION

Away Supporters' Entrances & Sections:
South West corner entrances for Rous Stand Lower

ADMISSION INFO (1998/99 PRICES)

Adult Seating: £14.00 – £16.00
Child Seating: £10.00 – £16.00
Note: Additional discounts available in Family Stand
Programme Price: £2.00

DISABLED INFORMATION

Wheelchairs: 40 spaces in total in the disabled sections, South East Corner and North Stand
Helpers: One helper admitted per disabled person
Prices: £6.00 for the disabled. £14.00 for helpers
Disabled Toilets: Adjacent to disabled enclosures Commentaries available in East Stand – no charge
Are Bookings Necessary: No
Contact: (01923) 496010

Travelling Supporters' Information:
Routes: From the North: Exit the M1 at Junction 5 and take the new road A4008 towards Watford Town Centre. This will take you round the ring road, follow signs for Watford General Hospital. The ground is next to the hospital; From the South: Exit the M1 at Junction 5 (then as North); From the East: Exit M25 at Junction 21A and join the M1 at Junction 6. Exit at Junction 5 (then as North); From the West: Exit the M25 at Junction 19 and take the third exit off the roundabout onto A411 (Hempstead Road) signposted for Watford. Continue for approximately two miles and go straight on at the roundabout (enter right-hand lane) for next roundabout and take the third exit into Rickmansworth Road. Take the second turning on the left into Cassio Road. Continue through the traffic lights into Merton Road and follow signs for Watford General Hospital into Vicarage Road.

WEST BROMWICH ALBION FC

Founded: 1879 (**Entered League**: 1888)	**Colours**: Shirts – Navy blue/white stripes
Former Names: West Bromwich Strollers	Shorts – White
(1879-1880)	**Telephone Nº**: (0121) 525-8888
Nickname: 'Throstles' 'Baggies' 'Albion'	**Ticket Office**: (0121) 553-5472
Ground: The Hawthorns, Halfords Lane,	**Fax Number**: (0121) 553-6634
West Bromwich, West Midlands B71 4LF	**Pitch Size**: 115 × 74 yards
Record Attendance: 64,815 (6/3/37)	**Ground Capacity**: 25,200 (All seats)

SMETHWICK END (Away)

WEST BROMWICH BUILDING SOCIETY FAMILY STAND

HALFORDS LANE MAIN STAND

BIRMINGHAM ROAD END

GENERAL INFORMATION

Supporters Club: c/o Alan Cleverley, 1 St. Christophers, Hamstead Hill, Handsworth Wood, Birmingham B20 1BP
Telephone Nº: (0121) 551-6439
Car Parking: Halfords Lane Car Parks, W.B.B.S. Stand Car Park
Coach Parking: W.B.B.S. Stand Car Park
Nearest Railway Station: Rolfe Street, Smethwick (1½ miles), Hawthorns (200 yards)
Nearest Bus Station: Town Centre
Club Shop: At Ground
Opening Times: Weekdays 9.00am – 5.30pm and Saturday Matchdays 9.00am – 2.45pm
Telephone Nº: (0121) 525-2145
Postal Sales: Yes
Nearest Police Station: Holyhead Road, Handsworth (° mile)
Police Telephone Nº: (0121) 554-3414

GROUND INFORMATION

Away Supporters' Entrances & Sections: Smethwick End 'A' turnstiles

ADMISSION INFO (1998/99 PRICES)
Adult Seating: £13.00 – £18.00
Child Seating: £6.50 – £11.00
Note: Additional discounts are available for advanced bookings
Programme Price: £1.50

DISABLED INFORMATION
Wheelchairs: 113 spaces in total in the disabled sections, Birmingham Road End & Smethwick End
Helpers: One helper admitted per disabled person
Prices: Free of charge for disabled. Helpers £13.00
Disabled Toilets: Available within disabled section Commentaries available for 6 people
Are Bookings Necessary: Yes
Contact: (0121) 525-8888

Travelling Supporters' Information:
Routes: From All Parts: Exit M5 at Junction 1 and follow Matchday signs for the ground. New traffic plan has made the "obvious" route via A41 unusable on matchdays.

WEST HAM UNITED FC

Founded: 1895 (**Entered League**: 1919)	**Colours**: Shirts – Claret and Blue
Former Names: Thames Iron Works FC	Shorts – White
Nickname: 'Hammers'	**Telephone Nº**: (0181) 548-2748
Ground: Boleyn Ground, Green Street,	**Ticket Office**: (0181) 548-2700
Upton Park, London E13 9AZ	**Fax Number**: (0181) 548-2758
Record Attendance: 42,322 (17/10/70)	**Pitch Size**: 112 × 72 yards
	Ground Capacity: 26,014 (All seats)

CASTLE STREET
BOBBY MOORE STAND

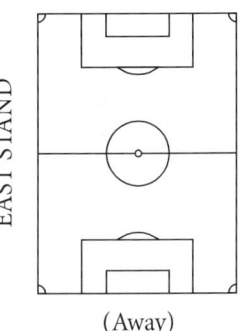

PRIORY ROAD EAST STAND

GREEN STREET WEST STAND

(Away)
CENTENARY STAND

GENERAL INFORMATION

Supporters Club: c/o Mr C. Rogers, West Ham Supporters' Club, Castle Street, East Ham, London E6 1PP
Telephone Nº: (0181) 472-1680
Car Parking: Street Parking
Coach Parking: By Police direction
Nearest Railway Station: Barking
Nearest Tube Station: Upton Park (5 minutes walk)
Club Shop: The Hammers Shop
Opening Times: Weekdays and Matchdays 9.30am – 5.00pm
Telephone Nº: (0181) 548-2748
Postal Sales: Yes
Nearest Police Station: East Ham High Street South (° mile)
Police Telephone Nº: (0181) 593-8232

GROUND INFORMATION

Away Supporters' Entrances & Sections:
Turnstiles 1a – 6, Centenary Stand

ADMISSION INFO (1998/99 PRICES)
Adult Seating: £18.00 – £31.00
Child Seating: £9.00 – £14.00
Note: Prices vary according to the category of game
Programme Price: £2.00

DISABLED INFORMATION
Wheelchairs: 16 spaces for home fans, 4 spaces for away fans in the disabled area, West Stand
Helpers: Admitted
Prices: Free of charge for disabled. Helpers £5.00
Disabled Toilets: One available 50 yards from the disabled area
Are Bookings Necessary: Yes
Contact: (0181) 548-2748

Travelling Supporters' Information:
Routes: From North and West: Take North Circular (A406) to A124 (East Ham) then along Barking Road for approximately 1½ miles until approaching traffic lights at crossroad. Turn right into Green Street, the ground is on the right-hand side; From South: Take the Blackwall Tunnel and A13 to Canning Town. Follow signs for East Ham (A124). After 1¾ miles turn left into Green Street; From East: Take A13 and turn right onto A117 at crossroads. After approximately 1 mile turn left at crossroads onto A124. Turn right (¾ mile) into Green Street.

WIGAN ATHLETIC FC

Founded: 1932 **(Entered League:** 1978)
Former Names: None
Nickname: 'Latics'
Ground: Springfield Park, Wigan, Lancs.
WN6 7BA
Record Attendance: 27,526 (12/12/53)
Pitch Size: 114 × 72 yards

Colours: Shirts – Blue, White and Green
Shorts – Blue
Telephone Nº: (01942) 244433
Ticket Office: (01942) 244433
Fax Number: (01942) 494654
Ground Capacity: 7,290
Seating Capacity: 1,128

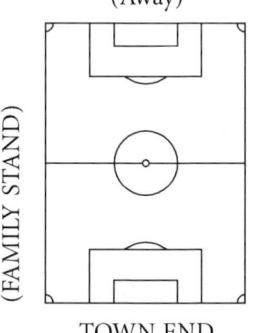

SHEVINGTON END
(Away)

PHOENIX STAND
(FAMILY STAND)

ST. ANDREWS DRIVE
POPULAR SIDE

TOWN END

GENERAL INFORMATION

Supporters Club: Joe Mills, c/o The Club
Telephone Nº: (01942) 243512
Car Parking: Street Parking
Coach Parking: Shevington End
Nearest Railway Station: Wallgate and Wigan
North Western (1 mile)
Nearest Bus Station: Wigan
Club Shop: At JJB Sports, Wigan and at the ground
Opening Times: Weekdays and Matchdays 9.00am
– 5.00pm
Nearest Police Station: Harrogate Street (1 mile)
Police Telephone Nº: (0161) 872-5050

GROUND INFORMATION

Away Supporters' Entrances & Sections:
Shevington End (open)

ADMISSION INFO (1998/99 PRICES)

Adult Standing: £7.50
Adult Seating: £10.00
Child Standing: £4.00
Child Seating: £6.00 (£5.00 in the Family Stand)
Programme Price: £1.80

DISABLED INFORMATION

Wheelchairs: 10 spaces in total for Home and Away
fans in the disabled section, Family Enclosure
Helpers: One helper admitted per disabled person
Prices: Free of charge for Disabled and Helpers
Disabled Toilets: Near the Family Enclosure
Commentaries are available in the Phoenix Stand
Are Bookings Necessary: Yes
Contact: (01942) 244433

Travelling Supporters' Information:
Routes: From North: Exit M6 at Junction 27 following signs for Wigan (A5209), turn right (¼ mile) (B5206).
Turn left after 1 mile and after 4½ miles take left turn into Springfield Road; From South: Exit M6 at Junction 25
following signs for Wigan (A49). Turn left into Robin Park Road and into Scot Lane. Turn right at the 3rd traffic
lights into Woodhouse Lane and left at the traffic lights into Springfield Road; From East: Take A557 into Town
Centre then left into Robin Park Road (then as South).

WIMBLEDON FC

Founded: 1889 (**Entered League**: 1977)
Former Names: Wimbledon Old Centrals
FC (1889-1905)
Nickname: 'Dons'
Ground: Selhurst Park, London
SE25 6PY
Record Attendance: 30,115 (1992-93)

Colours: Shirts – Blue
Shorts – Blue
Telephone Nº: (0181) 771-2233
Ticket Office: (0181) 771-8841
Fax Number: (0181) 768-0640
Pitch Size: 110 × 74 yards
Ground Capacity: 26,296 (All seats)

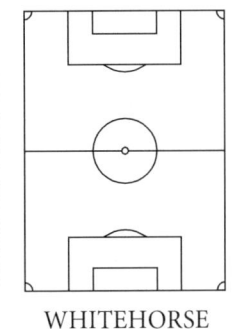

HOLMESDALE ROAD STAND

PARK ROAD (Away) ARTHUR WAIT STAND

CLIFTON ROAD MAIN STAND

WHITEHORSE LANE STAND

GENERAL INFORMATION
Supporters Club: Peter Tilbrook, c/o The Club
Telephone Nº: (0181) 771-2233
Car Parking: Street Parking
Coach Parking: Thornton Heath
Nearest Railway Station: Selhurst/Norwood
Junction (5 minutes walk)
Nearest Bus Station: Norwood Junction
Club Shop: At Ground
Opening Times: Weekdays and Matchdays 9.30am
–5.30pm
Telephone Nº: (0181) 768-6100
Postal Sales: Yes
Nearest Police Station: South Norwood
(15 minutes walk)
Police Telephone Nº: (0181) 653-8568

GROUND INFORMATION
Away Supporters' Entrances & Sections:
Park Road turnstiles for Arthur Wait Stand

ADMISSION INFO (1998/99 PRICES)
Adult Seating: £10.00 – £25.00
Child Seating: £5.00 – £10.00
Note: Prices vary according to category of match
and ground position
Programme Price: £2.00

DISABLED INFORMATION
Wheelchairs: Unconfirmed number accommo-
dated in the disabled area, Holmesdale Road Stand
Helpers: One helper admitted per disabled person
Prices: Free for the disabled. Concessionary prices
for helpers
Disabled Toilets: Located in the disabled area
Commentaries are available for 12 people
Are Bookings Necessary: Yes
Contact: (0181) 771-8841

Travelling Supporters' Information:
Routes: From North: Take M1/A1 to North Circular (A406) to Chiswick. Then take the South Circular (A205) to Wandsworth and then the A3 to the A214 and follow signs to Streatham to the A23. Turn left onto the B273 after 1 mile, follow to the end and turn left into the High Street and into Whitehorse Lane; From East: Take A232 (Croydon Road) to Shirley and join A215 (Northwood Road). After 2¼ miles turn left into Whitehorse Lane; From South: Take A23 and follow signs for Crystal Palace (B266) through Thornton Heath into Whitehorse Lane; From West: Take the M4 to Chiswich (then as North).

WOLVERHAMPTON WANDERERS FC

Founded: 1877 (**Entered League:** 1888)
Former Names: St. Luke's FC & The
Wanderers FC (combined in 1880)
Nickname: 'Wolves'
Ground: Molineux Stadium, Waterloo
Road, Wolverhampton WV1 4QR
Record Attendance: 61,315 (11/2/39)

Colours: Shirts – Gold
Shorts – Black
Telephone Nº: (01902) 655000
Ticket Office: (01902) 653653
Fax Number: (01902) 687006
Pitch Size: 110 × 75 yards
Ground Capacity: 28,500 (All seats)

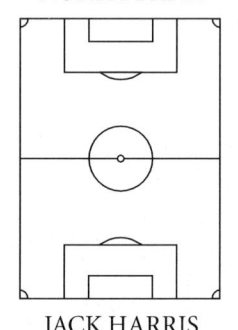

STAN CULLIS STAND
NORTH BANK

WATERLOO ROAD
BILLY WRIGHT STAND

MOLINEUX STREET
JOHN IRELAND STAND

JACK HARRIS
STAND

GENERAL INFORMATION

Supporters Club: c/o Consumer Sales Dept, Molineux
Stadium, Waterloo Road, Wolverhampton WV1 4QR
Telephone Nº: (01902) 656100
Car Parking: Around West Park, Newhampton Road
& rear of Stan Cullis Stand + Town Centre (5 mins.)
Coach Parking: By Police direction
Nearest Railway Station: Wolverhampton (1 mile)
Nearest Bus Station: Wolverhampton (¼ mile)
Club Shop: At ground and in Town Centre
Opening Times: Daily 9.00am – 5.00pm
Telephone Nº: (01902) 687032
Postal Sales: Yes (Phone (01902) 658800)
Nearest Police Station: Bilston St., Wolverhampton
Police Telephone Nº: (01902) 649000

GROUND INFORMATION

Away Supporters' Entrances & Sections:
Jack Harris turnstiles for Block 5 or John Ireland
Stand Lower Tier (turnstiles for Block 3)

ADMISSION INFO (1998/99 PRICES)

Adult Seating: £12.00 – £17.00
Child Seating: £8.50 – £11.00
Note: Members receive ticket discounts and other
concessions in the Family Area.
Programme Price: £1.50

DISABLED INFORMATION

Wheelchairs: 120 spaces in total for Home and Away
fans in the disabled sections, Stan Cullis Stand and
Billy Wright Family Enclosure
Helpers: One helper admitted per wheelchair
Prices: Free of charge for disabled. Helpers £6.00
Disabled Toilets: Toilets at both end of the Stand
Cullis Stand
Commentaries by a local blind organisation
Are Bookings Necessary: Yes
Contact: (01902) 658666 (Tracey Lilley)

Travelling Supporters' Information:
Routes: From North: Exit M6 Junction 12. At island take 3rd exit onto A5 for Wolverhampton. At next island turn left onto A449.
After 6 miles A449 passes under M54, carry straight on and at 6th roundabout (Five Ways) take 3rd exit into Waterloo Road.
Molineux is 1 mile straight on; From South/West: Exit M5 Junction 2, follow signs for Wolverhampton on A4123 for 8 miles to
ring road. Turn left on ring road (follow Molineux Centre signs). Take 2nd exit at next 2 islands * Pass Bank's Brewery and Swim-
ming Baths on left and turn left at next set of traffic lights. Molineux is 500 yards on right; From East: Exit M6 Junction 10, take
A454 (via Willenhall) to Wolverhampton ring road. At first ring road island take 4th exit (A449 to Stafford). Straight on at next 2
sets of traffic lights. Filter right at third set of lights (Waterloo Road). Molineux is 500 yards on right; From West: Take A41 to
Wolverhampton ring road roundabout. Turn left into the ring road. Then as from South/West *

WREXHAM AFC

Founded: 1873 (**Entered League:** 1921)
Former Names: None
Nickname: 'Robins'
Ground: Racecourse Ground, Mold Road, Wrexham, North Wales LL11 2AH
Record Attendance: 34,445 (26/1/57)
Pitch Size: 111 × 71 yards

Colours: Shirts – Red
Shorts – White
Telephone Nº: (01978) 262129
Ticket Office: (01978) 262129
Fax Number: (01978) 357821
Ground Capacity: 11,500
Seating Capacity: 5,026

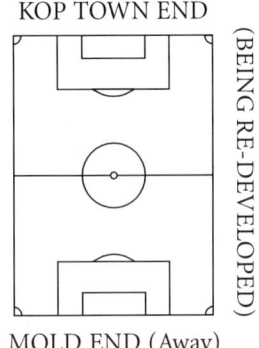

CRISPIN LANE
KOP TOWN END
(CAR PARK) YALE STAND
MOLD ROAD STAND (BEING RE-DEVELOPED)
MOLD END (Away)
MARSTONS STAND

GENERAL INFORMATION
Supporters Club: Miss Ena Williams, c/o The Club
Telephone Nº: (01978) 262129
Car Parking: Town car parks nearby + Newi College (Mold End)
Coach Parking: –
Nearest Railway Station: Wrexham General (adjacent)
Nearest Bus Station: Wrexham (King Street)
Club Shop: Promotions Office, at the Ground
Opening Times: Office hours only
Telephone Nº: (01978) 352536
Postal Sales: Yes
Nearest Police Station: Bodhyfryd (HQ) (1 mile)
Police Telephone Nº: (01978) 290222

GROUND INFORMATION
Away Supporters' Entrances & Sections:
Mold End turnstiles for Marstons Stand and Marstons Paddock (both covered)

ADMISSION INFO (1998/99 PRICES)
Adult Standing: £9.00
Adult Seating: £11.00 – £12.00
Child Standing: £5.00
Child Seating: £7.00
Programme Price: £1.80

DISABLED INFORMATION
Wheelchairs: 18 spaces in total for Home and Away fans in the disabled section, Mold Road Side
Helpers: One helper admitted per wheelchair
Prices: Free of charge for disabled. Helpers £7.00
Disabled Toilets: Available in the disabled section
Are Bookings Necessary: Yes
Contact: (01978) 351332 (Tony Millington)

Travelling Supporters' Information:
Routes: From the North and West: Take A483 and Wrexham bypass to junction with A541. Branch left at the roundabout and follow Wrexham signs into Mold Road; From the East: Take A525 or A534 into Wrexham then follow A541 signs into Mold Road; From the South: Take the M6, then M54 and follow the A5 and A483 to the Wrexham bypass and the junction with the A541. Branch right at the roundabout and follow Town Centre signs.

WYCOMBE WANDERERS FC

Founded: 1884 (**Entered League**: 1993)
Former Names: None
Nickname: 'The Blues'; 'The Chairboys'
Ground: Adams Park, Hillbottom Road,
Sands, High Wycombe, Bucks
Record Attendance: 9,007 (7/1/95)
Pitch Size: 115 × 75 yards

Colours: Shirts – Dark/light blue quarters
Shorts – Navy blue
Telephone Nº: (01494) 472100
Ticket Office: (01494) 441118
Fax Number: (01494) 527633
Ground Capacity: 10,000
Seating Capacity: 7,306

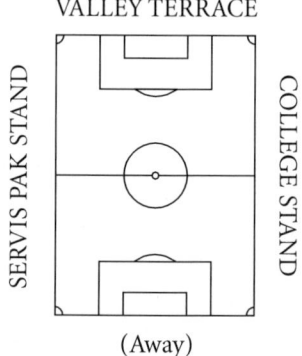

VALLEY TERRACE

SERVIS PAK STAND

AMERSHAM & WYCOMBE COLLEGE STAND

(Away)
ROGER VERE END

GENERAL INFORMATION

Supporters Club: None
Telephone Nº: –
Car Parking: Car park at the ground (302 cars)
Coach Parking: Car park at the ground
Nearest Railway Station: High Wycombe
Nearest Bus Station: High Wycombe
Club Shop: At the ground and also in Town
Opening Times: Weekdays and Matchdays
Telephone Nº: (01494) 472100 (Ground Shop);
(01494) 450957 (Town Shop)
Postal Sales: Yes
Nearest Police Station: Queen Victoria Road, High
Wycombe (2½ miles)
Police Telephone Nº: (01494) 465888

GROUND INFORMATION

Away Supporters' Entrances & Sections:
Roger Vere Stand entrances and accommodation

ADMISSION INFO (1998/99 PRICES)

Adult Standing: £10.00
Adult Seating: £13.00 – £15.00
Child Standing: £6.00 – £7.00
Child Seating: £6.00 (Family Stand); £8.00 –
£13.00 elsewhere
Note: Discounts available on advanced bookings
Programme Price: £2.00

DISABLED INFORMATION

Wheelchairs: 50 spaces in total available in the
disabled section of the Family Stand
Helpers: One helper admitted per wheelchair
Prices: £6.00 for the disabled. Full price for helpers
Disabled Toilets: Available in the New Family Stand
Commentaries are available for 5 people
Are Bookings Necessary: Yes
Contact: (01494) 472100

Travelling Supporters' Information:
Routes: From All Parts: Exit M40 at Junction 4 and take A4010 following Aylesbury signs. Go straight on at 3 mini-roundabouts and bear sharp left at 4th roundabout into Lane End Road. Fork right into Hillbottom Road at the next roundabout. The ground is at the end of the road. Hillbottom Road is on the Sands Industrial Estate; From Town Centre: Take A40 West and after 1½ miles turn left into Chapel Lane (after the traffic lights). Turn right then right again at the mini-roundabout into Lane End Road – then as above.

YORK CITY FC

Founded: 1922 (**Entered League:** 1929)	**Colours:** Shirts – Red
Former Names: None	Shorts – Blue
Nickname: 'Minstermen'	**Telephone Nº:** (01904) 624447
Ground: Bootham Crescent, York	**Ticket Office:** (01904) 624447
YO30 7AQ	**Fax Number:** (01904) 631457
Record Attendance: 28,123 (5/3/38)	**Ground Capacity:** 9,534
Pitch Size: 115 × 74 yards	**Seating Capacity:** 3,509

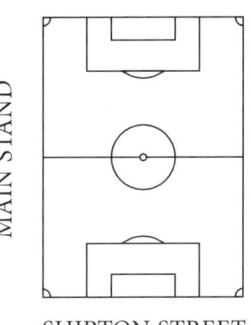

BOOTHAM CRESCENT (Away)
GROSVENOR ROAD END

MAIN STAND

POPULAR STAND

SHIPTON STREET

GENERAL INFORMATION

Supporters Club: c/o Raymond Wynn, 155 Manor Drive North, York
Telephone Nº: (01904) 797578
Car Parking: Street Parking
Coach Parking: By Police direction
Nearest Railway Station: York (1 mile)
Nearest Bus Station: York
Club Shop: At Ground
Opening Times: Monday to Wednesday 9.00am – 5.00pm; Thursday 9.00am – 5.00pm; Friday 9.00am – 4.30pm; Saturday Matches 1.00–3.00 & 4.40–5.30
Telephone Nº: (01904) 645941
Postal Sales: Yes
Nearest Police Station: Fulford
Police Telephone Nº: (01904) 631321

GROUND INFORMATION

Away Supporters' Entrances & Sections:
Grosvenor Road turnstiles for Grosvenor Road End

ADMISSION INFO (1998/99 PRICES)

Adult Standing: £8.00
Adult Seating: £9.00 – £11.00
Child Standing: £5.00
Child Seating: £6.00 – £7.00
Note: Additional concessions available in Family Stand
Programme Price: £1.80

DISABLED INFORMATION

Wheelchairs: 18 spaces in total for Home and Away fans in the disabled section, in front of Family Stand
Helpers: One helper admitted per disabled person
Prices: Free of charge for disabled. Helpers £8.50
Disabled Toilets: Available at entrance to the disabled area
Commentaries are available for the blind
Are Bookings Necessary: No
Contact: (01904) 624447

Travelling Supporters' Information:
Routes: From North: Take A1 then A59 following York signs. Cross railway bridge and turn left after 2 miles into Water End. Turn right at the end following City Centre signs for nearly ½ mile then turn left into Bootham Crescent; From South: Take A64 and turn left after Buckles Inn onto Outer Ring Road. Turn right onto A19, follow City Centre signs for 1½ miles then turn left into Bootham Crescent; From East: Take Outer Ring Road turning left onto A19. Then as South; From West: Take Outer Ring Road turning right onto A19. Then as South.

F.A. Carling Premier League Season 1997/98	Arsenal	Aston Villa	Barnsley	Blackburn Rovers	Bolton Wanderers	Chelsea	Coventry City	Crystal Palace	Derby County	Everton	Leeds United	Leicester City	Liverpool	Manchester United	Newcastle United	Sheffield Wednesday	Southampton	Tottenham Hotspur	West Ham United	Wimbledon
Arsenal	■	0-0	5-0	1-3	4-1	2-0	2-0	1-0	1-0	4-0	2-1	2-1	0-1	3-2	3-1	1-0	3-0	0-0	4-0	5-0
Aston Villa	1-0	■	0-1	0-4	1-3	0-2	3-0	3-1	2-1	2-1	1-0	1-1	2-1	0-2	0-1	2-2	1-1	4-1	2-0	1-2
Barnsley	0-2	0-3	■	1-1	2-1	0-6	2-0	1-0	1-0	2-2	2-3	0-2	2-3	0-2	2-2	2-1	4-3	1-1	1-2	2-1
Blackburn Rovers	1-4	5-0	2-1	■	3-1	1-0	0-0	2-2	1-0	3-2	3-4	5-3	1-1	1-3	1-0	7-2	1-0	0-3	3-0	0-0
Bolton Wanderers	0-1	0-1	1-1	2-1	■	1-0	1-5	5-2	3-3	0-0	2-3	2-0	1-1	0-0	1-0	3-2	0-0	1-1	1-1	1-0
Chelsea	2-3	0-1	2-0	0-1	2-0	■	3-1	6-2	4-0	2-0	0-0	1-0	4-1	0-1	1-0	1-0	4-2	2-0	2-1	1-1
Coventry City	2-2	1-2	1-0	2-0	2-2	3-2	■	1-1	1-0	0-0	0-0	0-2	1-1	3-2	2-2	1-0	1-0	4-0	1-1	0-0
Crystal Palace	0-0	1-1	0-1	1-2	2-2	0-3	0-3	■	3-1	1-3	0-2	0-3	0-3	0-3	1-2	1-0	1-1	1-3	3-3	0-3
Derby County	3-0	0-1	1-0	3-1	4-0	0-1	3-1	0-0	■	3-1	0-5	0-4	1-0	2-2	1-0	3-0	4-0	2-1	2-0	1-1
Everton	2-2	1-4	4-2	1-0	3-2	3-1	1-1	1-2	1-2	■	2-0	1-1	2-0	0-2	0-0	1-3	0-2	0-2	2-1	0-0
Leeds United	1-1	1-1	2-1	4-0	2-0	3-1	3-3	0-2	4-3	0-0	■	0-1	0-2	1-0	4-1	1-2	0-1	1-0	3-1	1-1
Leicester City	3-3	1-0	1-0	1-1	0-0	2-0	1-1	1-1	1-2	0-1	1-0	■	0-0	0-0	0-0	1-1	3-3	3-0	2-1	0-1
Liverpool	4-0	3-0	0-1	0-0	2-1	4-2	1-0	2-1	4-0	1-1	3-1	1-2	■	1-3	1-0	2-1	2-3	4-0	5-0	2-0
Manchester United	0-1	1-0	7-0	4-0	1-1	2-2	3-0	2-0	2-0	2-0	3-0	0-1	1-1	■	1-1	6-1	1-0	2-0	2-1	2-0
Newcastle United	0-1	1-0	2-1	1-1	2-1	3-1	0-0	1-2	0-0	1-0	1-1	3-3	1-2	0-1	■	2-1	2-1	1-0	0-1	1-3
Sheffield Wednes.	2-0	1-3	2-1	0-0	5-0	1-4	0-0	1-3	2-5	3-1	1-3	1-0	3-3	2-0	2-1	■	1-0	1-0	1-1	1-1
Southampton	1-3	1-2	4-1	3-0	0-1	1-0	1-2	1-0	0-2	2-1	0-2	2-1	1-1	1-0	2-1	2-3	■	3-2	3-0	0-1
Tottenham Hotspur	1-1	3-2	3-0	0-0	1-0	1-6	1-1	0-1	1-0	1-1	0-1	1-1	3-3	0-2	2-0	3-2	1-1	■	1-0	0-0
West Ham United	0-0	2-1	6-0	2-1	3-0	2-1	1-0	4-1	0-0	2-2	3-0	4-3	2-1	1-1	0-1	1-0	2-4	2-1	■	3-1
Wimbledon	0-1	2-1	4-1	0-1	0-0	0-2	1-2	0-1	0-0	0-0	1-0	2-1	1-1	2-5	0-0	1-1	1-0	2-6	1-2	■

Nationwide Division One Season 1997/98	Birmingham City	Bradford City	Bury	Charlton Athletic	Crewe Alexandra	Huddersfield Town	Ipswich Town	Manchester City	Middlesbrough	Norwich City	Nottingham Forest	Oxford United	Portsmouth	Port Vale	Queen's Park Rangers	Reading	Sheffield United	Stockport County	Stoke City	Sunderland	Swindon Town	Tranmere Rovers	West Bromwich Albion	Wolverhampton Wanderers
Birmingham City		0-0	1-3	0-0	0-1	0-0	1-1	2-1	1-1	1-2	1-2	0-0	2-1	1-1	1-0	3-0	2-0	4-1	2-0	0-1	3-0	0-0	1-0	1-0
Bradford City	0-0		1-0	1-0	1-1	2-1	2-1	2-2	2-1	0-3	0-0	1-3	2-1	1-1	4-1	1-1	2-1	0-0	0-4	1-1	0-1	0-0	2-0	
Bury	2-1	2-0		0-0	1-1	2-2	0-1	1-1	0-1	1-0	2-0	1-0	0-2	2-2	1-1	1-1	1-1	0-1	0-0	1-1	1-0	1-0	1-3	1-3
Charlton Athletic	1-1	4-1	0-0		3-2	1-0	3-0	2-1	3-0	2-1	4-2	3-2	1-0	1-0	1-1	3-0	2-1	1-3	1-1	1-1	3-0	2-0	5-0	1-0
Crewe Alexandra	0-2	5-0	1-2	0-3		2-5	0-0	1-0	1-1	1-0	1-4	2-1	3-1	0-1	2-3	1-0	2-1	0-1	2-0	0-3	2-0	2-1	2-3	0-2
Huddersfield Town	0-1	1-2	2-0	0-3	2-0		2-2	1-3	0-1	1-3	0-2	5-1	1-1	0-4	1-1	1-0	0-0	1-0	3-1	2-3	0-0	3-0	1-0	1-0
Ipswich Town	0-1	2-1	2-0	3-1	3-2	5-1		1-0	1-1	5-0	0-1	5-2	2-0	5-1	0-0	1-0	2-2	0-2	2-3	2-0	2-1	0-0	1-1	3-0
Manchester City	0-1	1-0	0-1	2-2	1-0	0-1	1-2		2-0	1-2	2-3	0-2	2-2	2-3	2-2	0-0	0-0	4-1	0-1	0-1	6-0	1-1	1-0	0-1
Middlesbrough	3-1	1-0	4-0	2-1	1-0	3-0	1-1	1-0		3-0	0-0	4-1	1-1	2-1	3-0	4-0	1-2	3-1	0-1	3-1	6-0	3-0	1-0	1-1
Norwich City	3-3	2-3	2-2	0-4	0-2	5-0	2-1	0-0	1-3		1-0	2-1	2-0	1-0	0-0	0-0	2-1	1-1	0-0	2-1	5-0	0-2	1-1	0-2
Nottingham Forest	1-0	2-2	3-0	5-2	3-1	3-0	2-1	1-3	4-0	4-1		1-3	2-1	4-0	1-0	3-0	2-1	1-0	0-3	3-0	2-2	1-0	3-0	
Oxford United	0-2	0-0	1-1	1-2	0-0	2-0	1-0	0-0	1-4	2-0	0-1		1-0	2-0	3-1	3-0	2-4	3-0	5-1	1-1	2-1	1-1	2-1	3-0
Portsmouth	1-1	1-1	1-1	0-2	2-3	3-0	0-1	0-3	0-0	1-1	0-1	2-1		3-1	3-1	0-2	1-1	1-0	2-0	1-4	0-1	1-0	2-3	3-2
Port Vale	0-1	0-0	1-1	0-1	2-3	4-1	1-3	2-1	0-1	2-2	0-1	3-0	2-1		2-0	0-0	0-0	2-1	0-0	3-1	0-1	0-1	1-2	0-2
Queen's Park Rng.	1-1	1-0	0-1	2-4	3-2	2-1	0-0	2-0	5-0	1-1	0-1	1-1	1-0	0-1		1-1	2-2	2-1	1-1	0-1	1-2	0-0	2-0	0-0
Reading	2-0	0-3	1-1	2-0	3-3	0-2	0-4	3-0	0-1	0-1	3-3	2-1	0-1	0-3	1-2		0-1	1-0	2-0	4-0	0-1	1-3	2-1	0-0
Sheffield United	0-0	2-1	3-0	4-1	1-0	1-1	0-1	1-1	1-0	2-2	1-0	1-0	2-1	2-1	2-2	4-0		5-1	3-2	2-0	2-1	2-1	2-4	1-0
Stockport County	2-2	1-2	0-0	3-0	0-1	3-0	0-1	3-1	1-1	2-2	2-2	3-2	3-1	3-0	2-0	5-1	1-0		1-0	1-1	4-2	3-1	2-1	1-0
Stoke City	0-7	2-1	3-2	1-2	0-2	1-2	1-1	2-5	1-2	2-0	1-1	0-0	2-1	2-1	2-1	1-2	2-2	2-1		1-2	1-2	0-3	0-0	3-0
Sunderland	1-1	2-0	2-1	0-0	2-1	3-1	2-2	3-1	1-2	0-1	1-1	3-1	2-1	4-2	2-2	4-1	4-2	4-1	3-0		0-0	3-0	2-0	1-1
Swindon Town	1-1	1-0	3-1	0-1	2-0	1-1	0-2	1-3	1-2	1-0	0-0	4-1	0-1	4-2	3-1	0-2	1-1	1-1	1-0	1-2		2-1	0-2	0-0
Tranmere Rovers	0-3	3-1	0-0	2-2	0-3	1-0	1-1	0-0	0-2	2-0	0-0	0-2	2-2	1-2	2-1	6-0	3-3	3-0	3-1	0-2	3-0		0-0	2-1
West Brom. Albion	1-0	1-1	1-1	1-0	0-1	0-2	2-3	0-1	2-1	1-0	1-1	1-2	0-3	2-2	1-1	1-0	2-0	3-2	1-1	3-3	0-0	2-1		1-0
Wolverhampton W.	1-3	2-1	4-2	3-1	1-0	1-1	1-1	2-2	1-0	5-0	2-1	1-0	2-0	1-1	3-2	3-1	0-0	3-4	1-1	0-1	3-1	2-1	0-0	

Nationwide Division Two — Season 1997/98

	Blackpool	Bournemouth	Brentford	Bristol City	Bristol Rovers	Burnley	Carlisle United	Chesterfield	Fulham	Gillingham	Grimsby Town	Luton Town	Millwall	Northampton Town	Oldham Athletic	Plymouth Argyle	Preston North End	Southend United	Walsall	Watford	Wigan Athletic	Wrexham	Wycombe Wanderers	York City
Blackpool	■	1-0	1-2	2-2	1-0	2-1	2-1	2-1	2-1	2-1	2-2	1-0	3-0	1-1	2-2	0-0	2-1	3-0	1-0	1-1	0-2	1-2	2-4	1-0
Bournemouth	2-0	■	0-0	1-0	1-1	2-1	3-2	2-0	2-1	4-0	0-1	1-1	0-0	3-0	0-0	3-3	0-2	2-1	1-0	0-1	1-0	0-1	0-0	0-0
Brentford	3-1	3-2	■	1-4	2-3	2-1	0-1	0-0	0-2	2-0	3-1	2-2	2-1	0-0	2-1	3-1	0-0	1-1	3-0	1-2	0-2	1-1	1-1	1-2
Bristol City	2-0	1-1	2-2	■	2-0	3-1	1-0	1-0	0-2	0-2	4-1	3-0	4-1	0-0	1-0	2-1	2-1	1-0	2-1	1-1	3-0	1-1	3-1	2-1
Bristol Rovers	0-3	5-3	2-1	1-2	■	1-0	3-1	3-1	2-3	1-2	0-4	2-1	2-1	0-2	3-1	1-1	2-2	2-0	2-0	1-2	5-0	1-0	3-1	1-2
Burnley	1-2	2-2	1-1	1-0	0-0	■	3-1	0-0	2-1	0-0	2-1	1-1	1-2	2-1	0-0	2-1	1-1	1-0	2-1	2-0	0-2	1-2	2-2	7-2
Carlisle United	1-1	0-1	1-2	0-3	3-1	2-1	■	0-2	2-0	2-1	0-1	0-1	1-0	0-2	3-1	2-2	0-2	5-0	1-1	0-2	1-0	2-2	0-0	1-2
Chesterfield	1-1	1-1	0-0	1-0	0-0	1-0	2-1	■	0-2	1-1	1-0	0-0	3-1	2-1	2-1	3-2	1-0	3-1	0-1	2-3	3-1	1-0	1-0	1-1
Fulham	1-0	0-1	1-1	1-0	1-0	1-0	5-0	1-1	■	3-0	0-2	0-0	1-2	1-1	3-1	2-0	2-1	2-0	1-1	1-2	2-0	1-0	0-0	1-1
Gillingham	1-1	2-1	3-1	2-0	1-1	2-0	1-0	1-0	2-0	■	0-2	2-1	1-3	1-0	2-1	2-1	0-0	1-2	2-1	2-2	0-0	1-1	1-0	0-0
Grimsby Town	1-0	2-1	4-0	1-1	1-2	4-1	1-0	0-0	1-1	0-0	■	0-1	0-1	1-0	0-2	1-0	3-1	5-1	3-0	0-1	2-1	0-0	0-0	0-0
Luton Town	3-0	1-2	2-0	0-0	2-4	2-3	3-2	3-0	1-4	2-2	2-2	■	0-2	2-2	1-1	3-0	1-3	1-0	0-1	0-4	1-1	2-5	0-0	3-0
Millwall	2-1	1-2	3-0	0-2	1-1	1-0	1-1	1-1	1-1	1-0	0-1	0-2	■	0-0	2-1	1-1	0-1	3-1	0-1	1-1	1-1	0-1	1-0	2-3
Northampton Town	2-0	0-2	4-0	2-1	1-1	0-1	2-1	0-0	1-0	2-1	2-1	1-0	2-0	■	0-0	2-1	2-2	3-1	3-2	0-1	1-0	0-1	2-0	1-1
Oldham Athletic	0-1	2-1	1-1	1-2	4-4	3-3	3-1	2-0	1-0	3-1	2-0	2-1	1-1	2-2	■	2-0	1-0	2-0	0-0	2-2	3-1	3-0	0-1	3-1
Plymouth Argyle	3-1	3-0	0-0	2-0	1-2	2-2	2-1	1-1	1-4	0-1	2-2	0-2	3-0	1-3	0-2	■	2-0	2-3	2-1	0-1	3-2	2-0	4-2	0-0
Preston North End	3-3	0-1	2-1	2-1	1-2	2-3	0-3	0-0	3-1	1-3	2-0	1-0	2-1	1-0	1-1	0-1	■	1-0	0-0	2-0	1-1	0-1	1-1	3-2
Southend United	2-1	5-3	3-1	0-2	1-1	1-0	1-1	0-2	1-0	0-0	0-1	1-2	0-0	0-0	1-1	3-0	3-2	■	0-1	0-3	1-0	1-3	1-2	4-4
Walsall	2-1	2-1	0-0	0-0	0-1	0-0	3-1	3-2	1-1	1-0	0-0	2-3	2-0	0-2	0-0	0-1	1-1	3-1	■	0-0	1-0	3-0	0-1	2-0
Watford	4-1	2-1	3-1	1-1	3-2	1-0	2-1	2-1	2-0	0-2	0-0	1-1	0-1	1-1	2-1	1-1	3-1	1-1	1-2	■	2-1	1-0	2-1	1-1
Wigan Athletic	3-0	1-0	4-0	0-3	3-0	5-1	0-2	2-1	2-1	1-4	0-2	1-1	0-0	1-1	1-0	1-1	1-4	1-3	2-0	3-2	■	3-2	5-2	1-1
Wrexham	3-4	2-1	2-2	2-1	1-0	0-0	2-2	0-0	0-3	0-0	0-0	2-1	1-0	1-0	3-1	1-1	0-0	3-1	2-1	1-1	2-2	■	2-0	1-2
Wycombe Wands.	2-1	1-1	0-0	1-2	1-0	2-1	1-4	1-1	2-0	1-0	1-1	2-2	0-0	0-0	2-1	5-1	0-0	4-1	4-2	0-0	1-2	0-0	■	1-0
York City	1-1	0-1	3-1	0-1	0-1	3-1	4-3	0-1	0-1	2-1	0-0	1-2	2-3	0-0	0-0	1-0	1-0	1-1	1-0	1-1	2-2	1-0	2-0	■

	Barnet	Brighton & Hove Alb.	Cambridge United	Cardiff City	Chester City	Colchester United	Darlington	Doncaster Rovers	Exeter City	Hartlepool United	Hull City	Leyton Orient	Lincoln City	Macclesfield Town	Mansfield Town	Notts County	Peterborough United	Rochdale	Rotherham United	Scarborough	Scunthorpe United	Shrewsbury Town	Swansea City	Torquay United
Barnet	■	2-0	2-0	2-2	2-1	3-2	2-0	1-1	1-2	1-1	2-0	1-2	0-0	3-1	0-1	1-2	2-0	3-1	0-0	1-1	0-1	1-1	2-0	3-3
Brighton & Hove Al.	0-3	■	0-2	0-1	3-2	4-1	0-0	0-0	1-3	0-0	2-2	0-1	0-1	1-1	1-1	0-1	2-2	2-1	1-2	1-1	2-1	0-0	0-1	1-4
Cambridge United	1-3	1-1	■	2-2	1-2	4-4	1-0	2-1	2-1	2-0	0-1	1-0	1-1	0-0	2-0	2-2	1-0	1-1	2-1	2-3	2-2	4-3	4-1	1-1
Cardiff City	1-1	0-0	0-0	■	0-2	0-2	0-0	7-1	1-1	1-1	2-1	1-0	0-1	1-2	4-1	1-1	0-0	2-1	2-2	1-1	0-0	2-2	0-1	1-1
Chester City	0-1	2-0	1-1	0-0	■	3-1	2-1	2-1	1-1	3-1	1-0	1-1	2-0	1-1	0-1	0-1	0-0	4-0	4-0	1-1	1-0	2-0	2-0	1-3
Colchester United	1-1	3-1	3-2	2-1	2-0	■	2-1	2-1	1-2	1-2	4-3	1-1	0-1	5-1	2-0	2-0	1-0	0-0	2-1	1-0	3-3	1-1	1-2	1-0
Darlington	2-3	1-0	1-1	0-0	1-0	4-2	■	5-1	3-2	1-1	4-3	1-0	2-2	4-2	0-0	0-2	3-1	1-0	1-1	1-2	1-0	3-1	3-2	1-2
Doncaster Rovers	0-2	1-3	0-0	1-1	2-1	0-1	0-2	■	0-1	2-2	1-0	1-4	2-4	0-3	0-3	1-2	0-5	0-3	0-3	1-2	1-2	1-0	0-3	0-1
Exeter City	0-0	2-1	1-0	1-1	5-0	0-1	1-0	5-1	■	1-1	3-0	2-2	1-2	1-3	1-0	2-5	0-0	3-0	3-1	1-1	2-3	2-2	1-0	1-1
Hartlepool United	2-0	0-0	3-3	2-0	0-0	3-2	2-2	3-1	1-1	■	2-2	2-2	1-1	0-0	2-2	1-1	2-1	2-0	0-0	3-0	0-1	2-1	4-2	3-0
Hull City	0-2	0-0	1-0	0-1	1-2	3-1	1-1	3-0	3-2	2-1	■	3-2	0-2	0-0	0-0	0-3	3-1	0-2	0-0	3-0	2-1	1-4	7-4	3-3
Leyton Orient	2-0	3-1	0-2	0-1	1-0	0-2	2-0	8-0	1-0	2-1	2-1	■	1-0	1-1	2-2	1-1	2-0	1-1	3-1	1-0	2-3	2-2	2-1	
Lincoln City	2-0	2-1	0-0	1-0	1-3	0-1	3-1	2-1	2-1	1-1	1-0	1-0	■	1-1	0-2	3-5	3-0	2-0	0-1	3-3	1-1	1-0	1-1	1-1
Macclesfield Town	2-0	1-0	3-1	1-0	3-2	0-0	2-1	3-0	2-2	2-1	2-0	1-0	1-0	■	1-0	2-0	1-1	1-0	3-1	2-0	2-1	3-0	2-1	
Mansfield Town	1-2	1-1	3-2	1-2	4-1	1-1	4-0	1-1	3-2	2-2	2-0	0-0	2-2	1-0	■	0-2	2-0	3-0	3-3	3-2	1-0	1-1	1-0	2-2
Notts County	2-0	2-2	1-0	3-1	1-2	0-0	1-1	5-2	1-1	2-0	1-0	1-0	1-2	1-1	1-0	■	2-2	2-1	5-2	1-0	2-1	1-1	2-1	3-0
Peterborough Utd.	5-1	1-2	1-0	2-0	2-1	3-2	1-1	0-1	1-1	0-0	2-0	2-0	5-1	0-1	1-1	1-0	■	3-1	1-0	0-0	0-1	1-1	3-1	2-0
Rochdale	2-1	2-0	2-0	0-0	1-1	2-1	5-0	4-1	3-0	2-1	2-1	0-2	0-0	2-0	2-0	1-2	1-2	■	0-1	4-0	2-0	3-1	3-0	0-1
Rotherham United	2-3	0-0	2-2	1-1	4-2	3-2	3-0	3-0	1-0	2-1	5-4	2-1	3-1	1-0	2-1	2-2	2-2		■	0-0	1-3	0-1	1-1	0-1
Scarborough	1-0	2-1	1-0	3-1	4-1	1-1	2-1	4-0	4-1	1-1	2-1	2-0	2-2	2-1	2-2	1-2	1-3	1-0	1-2	■	0-0	0-0	3-2	4-1
Scunthorpe United	1-1	0-2	3-3	3-3	2-1	1-0	1-0	1-1	2-1	1-1	2-0	1-0	0-1	1-0	1-0	1-2	1-3	2-0	1-1	1-3	■	1-1	1-0	2-0
Shrewsbury Town	2-0	2-1	1-1	3-2	1-1	0-2	3-0	2-1	1-1	1-0	2-0	1-2	0-2	4-3	3-2	1-2	4-1	1-0	2-1	0-1	0-2	■	0-1	1-2
Swansea City	0-2	1-0	1-1	1-1	2-0	0-1	4-0	0-0	2-1	0-2	2-0	1-1	0-0	1-1	0-1	1-2	0-1	3-0	1-1	0-0	2-0	0-1	■	2-0
Torquay United	0-0	3-0	0-3	1-0	3-1	1-1	2-1	2-0	1-2	1-0	5-1	1-1	3-2	2-0	2-1	0-2	3-1	0-0	1-2	1-0	2-4	3-0	2-0	■

F.A. Premier League

Season 1997/98

Arsenal	38	23	9	6	68	33	78
Manchester United	38	23	8	7	73	26	77
Liverpool	38	18	11	9	68	42	65
Chelsea	38	20	3	15	71	43	63
Leeds United	38	17	8	13	57	46	59
Blackburn Rovers	38	16	10	12	57	52	58
Aston Villa	38	17	6	15	49	48	57
West Ham United	38	16	8	14	56	57	56
Derby County	38	16	7	15	52	49	55
Leicester City	38	13	14	11	51	41	53
Coventry City	38	12	16	10	46	44	52
Southampton	38	14	6	18	50	55	48
Newcastle United	38	11	11	16	35	44	44
Tottenham Hotspur	38	11	11	16	44	56	44
Wimbledon	38	10	14	14	34	46	44
Sheffield Wednesday	38	12	8	18	52	67	44
Everton	38	9	13	16	41	56	40
Bolton Wanderers	38	9	13	16	41	61	40
Barnsley	38	10	5	23	37	82	35
Crystal Palace	38	8	9	21	37	71	33

Champions: Arsenal
Relegated: Crystal Palace, Barnsley and Bolton Wanderers

Football League Division One

Season 1997/98

Nottingham Forest	46	28	10	8	82	42	94
Middlesbrough	46	27	10	9	77	41	91
Sunderland	46	26	12	8	86	50	90
Charlton Athletic	46	26	10	10	80	49	88
Ipswich Town	46	23	14	9	77	43	83
Sheffield United	46	19	17	10	69	54	74
Birmingham City	46	19	17	10	60	35	74
Stockport County	46	19	8	19	71	69	65
Wolverhampton Wanderers	46	18	11	17	57	53	65
West Bromwich Albion	46	16	13	17	50	56	61
Crewe Alexandra	46	18	5	23	58	65	59
Oxford United	46	16	10	20	60	64	58
Bradford City	46	14	15	17	46	59	57
Tranmere Rovers	46	14	14	18	54	57	56
Norwich City	46	14	13	19	52	69	55
Huddersfield Town	46	14	11	21	50	72	53
Bury	46	11	19	16	42	58	52
Swindon Town	46	14	10	22	42	73	52
Port Vale	46	13	10	23	56	66	49
Portsmouth	46	13	10	23	51	63	49
Queen's Park Rangers	46	10	19	17	51	63	49
Manchester City	46	12	12	22	56	57	48
Stoke City	46	11	13	22	44	74	46
Reading	46	11	9	26	39	78	42

Promotion Play-offs

Ipswich Town	0	Charlton Athletic	1
Sheffield United	2	Sunderland	1

Charlton Athletic	1	Ipswich Town	0

Charlton Athletic won 2-0 on aggregate

Sunderland	2	Sheffield United	0

Sunderland won 3-2 on aggregate

Charlton Athletic	4	Sunderland	4

After extra time. Full-time 3-3. Charlton Athletic won 7-6 on penalties

Promoted: Nottingham Forest, Middlesbrough and Charlton Athletic

Relegated: Reading, Stoke City and Manchester City

Football League Division Two

Watford	46	24	16	6	67	41	88
Bristol City	46	25	10	11	69	39	85
Grimsby Town	46	19	15	12	55	37	72
Northampton Town	46	18	17	11	52	37	71
Bristol Rovers	46	20	10	16	70	64	70
Fulham	46	20	10	16	60	43	70
Wrexham	46	18	16	12	55	51	70
Gillingham	46	19	13	14	52	47	70
Bournemouth	46	18	12	16	57	52	66
Chesterfield	46	16	17	13	46	44	65
Wigan Athletic	46	17	11	18	64	66	62
Blackpool	46	17	11	18	59	67	62
Oldham Athletic	46	15	16	15	62	54	61
Wycombe Wanderers	46	14	18	14	51	53	60
Preston North End	46	15	14	17	56	56	59
York City	46	14	17	15	52	58	59
Luton Town	46	14	15	17	60	64	57
Millwall	46	14	13	19	43	54	55
Walsall	46	14	12	20	43	52	54
Burnley	46	13	13	20	55	65	52
Brentford	46	11	17	18	50	71	50
Plymouth Argyle	46	12	13	21	55	70	49
Carlisle United	46	12	8	26	57	73	44
Southend United	46	11	10	25	47	79	43

Promotion Play-offs

Fulham	1	Grimsby Town	1
Bristol Rovers	3	Northampton Town	1

Grimsby Town	1	Fulham	0

Grimsby Town won 2-1 on aggregate

Northampton Town	3	Bristol Rovers	0

Northampton Town won 4-3 on aggregate

Grimsby Town	1	Northampton Town	0

Promoted: Watford, Bristol City and Grimsby Town

Relegated: Southend United, Carlisle United, Plymouth Argyle and Brentford

Football League Division Three

Notts County	46	29	12	5	82	43	99
Macclesfield Town	46	23	13	10	63	44	82
Lincoln City	46	20	15	11	60	51	75
Colchester United	46	21	11	14	72	60	74
Torquay United	46	21	11	14	68	59	74
Scarborough	46	19	15	12	67	58	72
Barnet	46	19	13	14	61	51	70
Scunthorpe United	46	19	12	15	56	52	69
Rotherham United	46	16	19	11	67	61	67
Peterborough United	46	18	13	15	63	51	67
Leyton Orient	46	19	12	15	62	47	66*
Mansfield Town	46	16	17	13	64	55	65
Shrewsbury Town	46	16	13	17	61	62	61
Chester City	46	17	10	19	60	61	61
Exeter City	46	15	15	16	68	63	60
Cambridge United	46	14	18	14	63	57	60
Hartlepool United	46	12	23	11	61	53	59
Rochdale	46	17	7	22	56	55	58
Darlington	46	14	12	20	56	72	54
Swansea City	46	13	11	22	49	62	50
Cardiff City	46	9	23	14	48	52	50
Hull City	46	11	8	27	56	83	41
Brighton & Hove Albion	46	6	17	23	38	66	35
Doncaster Rovers	46	4	8	34	30	113	20

* Leyton Orient had 3 points deducted

Promotion Play-offs

Barnet	1	Colchester United	0
Scarborough	1	Torquay United	3

Colchester United	3	Barnet	1

Colchester United won 3-2 on aggregate

Torquay United	4	Scarborough	1

Torquay United won 7-2 on aggregate

Colchester United	1	Torquay United	0

Promoted: Notts County, Macclesfield Town, Lincoln City and Colchester United

Relegated: Doncaster Rovers

F.A. CUP 1997/98

First Round

15th Nov 1997	Barnet	1	Watford	2
15th Nov 1997	Billericay Town	2	Wisbech Town	3
15th Nov 1997	Blackpool	4	Blyth Spartans	3
15th Nov 1997	Bournemouth	3	Heybridge Swifts	0
15th Nov 1997	Brentford	2	Colchester United	2
15th Nov 1997	Bristol City	1	Millwall	0
14th Nov 1997	Bristol Rovers	2	Gillingham	2
15th Nov 1997	Carlisle United	0	Wigan Athletic	1
15th Nov 1997	Carshalton Athletic	0	Stevenage Borough	0
15th Nov 1997	Cheltenham Town	2	Tiverton Town	1
15th Nov 1997	Chester City	2	Winsford United	1
15th Nov 1997	Chesterfield	1	Northwich Victoria	0
15th Nov 1997	Darlington	1	Solihull Borough	1
15th Nov 1997	Exeter City	1	Northampton Town	1
15th Nov 1997	Farnborough Town	0	Dagenham & Redbridge	1
15th Nov 1997	Hartlepool United	2	Macclesfield Town	4
15th Nov 1997	Hayes	0	Boreham Wood	1
15th Nov 1997	Hendon	2	Leyton Orient	2
15th Nov 1997	Hereford United	2	Brighton & Hove Albion	1
15th Nov 1997	Hull City	0	Hednesford Town	2
15th Nov 1997	Ilkeston Town	2	Boston United	1
15th Nov 1997	King's Lynn	1	Bromsgrove Rovers	0
15th Nov 1997	Lincoln City	1	Gainsborough Trinity	1
15th Nov 1997	Luton Town	0	Torquay United	1
16th Nov 1997	Margate	1	Fulham	2
15th Nov 1997	Morecambe	1	Emley	1
16th Nov 1997	Notts County	2	Colwyn Bay	0
15th Nov 1997	Oldham Athletic	1	Mansfield Town	1
15th Nov 1997	Plymouth Argyle	0	Cambridge United	0
15th Nov 1997	Preston North End	3	Doncaster Rovers	2
15th Nov 1997	Rochdale	0	Wrexham	2
15th Nov 1997	Rotherham United	3	Burnley	3
15th Nov 1997	Scunthorpe United	2	Scarborough	1
15th Nov 1997	Shrewsbury Town	1	Grimsby Town	1
15th Nov 1997	Slough Town	1	Cardiff City	1
15th Nov 1997	Southport	0	York City	4
14th Nov 1997	Swansea City	1	Peterborough United	4
15th Nov 1997	Walsall	2	Lincoln United	0
15th Nov 1997	Woking	0	Southend United	2
15th Nov 1997	Wycombe Wanderers	2	Basingstoke	2

Replays

25th Nov 1997	Basingstoke	2	Wycombe Wanderers	2	(aet)

Basingstoke won 5-4 on penalties

25th Nov 1997	Burnley	0	Rotherham United	3	
25th Nov 1997	Cambridge United	3	Plymouth Argyle	2	(aet)
25th Nov 1997	Cardiff City	3	Slough Town	2	(aet)
25th Nov 1997	Colchester United	0	Brentford	0	(aet)

Colchester United won 4-2 on penalties

25th Nov 1997	Emley	3	Morecambe	3	(aet)

Emley won 3-1 on penalties

25th Nov 1997	Gillingham	0	Bristol Rovers	2	
25th Nov 1997	Grimsby Town	4	Shrewsbury Town	0	
25th Nov 1997	Leyton Orient	0	Hendon	1	
25th Nov 1997	Lincoln City	3	Gainsborough Trinity	2	
25th Nov 1997	Mansfield Town	0	Oldham Athletic	1	
25th Nov 1997	Northampton Town	2	Exeter City	1	
26th Nov 1997	Solihull Borough	3	Darlington	3	(aet)

Darlington won 4-2 on penalties

24th Nov 1997	Stevenage Borough	5	Carshalton Athletic	0	

Second Round

7th Dec 1997	Bournemouth	3	Bristol City	1
6th Dec 1997	Cambridge United	1	Stevenage Borough	1
6th Dec 1997	Cardiff City	3	Hendon	1
6th Dec 1997	Cheltenham Town	1	Boreham Wood	1
5th Dec 1997	Chester City	0	Wrexham	2
6th Dec 1997	Colchester United	1	Hereford United	1
6th Dec 1997	Fulham	1	Southend United	0
6th Dec 1997	Grimsby Town	2	Chesterfield	2
6th Dec 1997	Hednesford Town	0	Darlington	1
6th Dec 1997	Lincoln City	2	Emley	2
6th Dec 1997	Macclesfield Town	0	Walsall	7
6th Dec 1997	Northampton Town	1	Basingstoke	1
6th Dec 1997	Oldham Athletic	2	Blackpool	1
6th Dec 1997	Peterborough United	3	Dagenham & Redbridge	2
6th Dec 1997	Preston North End	2	Notts County	2
6th Dec 1997	Rotherham United	6	King's Lynn	0
6th Dec 1997	Scunthorpe United	1	Ilkeston Town	1
6th Dec 1997	Torquay United	1	Watford	1
6th Dec 1997	Wigan Athletic	2	York City	1
6th Dec 1997	Wisbech Town	0	Bristol Rovers	2

Replays

16th Dec 1997	Basingstoke	0	Northampton Town	0	(aet)

Northampton Town won 4-3 on penalties

16th Dec 1997	Boreham Wood	0	Cheltenham Town	2	
16th Dec 1997	Chesterfield	0	Grimsby Town	2	
17th Dec 1997	Emley	3	Lincoln City	3	(aet)

Emley won 4-3 on penalties

16th Dec 1997	Hereford United	1	Colchester United	1	(aet)

Hereford United won 5-4 on penalties

17th Dec 1997	Ilkeston Town	1	Scunthorpe United	2	
16th Dec 1997	Notts County	1	Preston North End	2	(aet)
15th Dec 1997	Stevenage Borough	2	Cambridge United	1	
16th Dec 1997	Watford	2	Torquay United	1	(aet)

Third Round

3rd Jan 1998	Arsenal	0	Port Vale	0
3rd Jan 1998	Barnsley	1	Bolton Wanderers	0
3rd Jan 1998	Blackburn Rovers	4	Wigan Athletic	2
13th Jan 1998	Bournemouth	0	Huddersfield Town	1
3rd Jan 1998	Bristol Rovers	1	Ipswich Town	1
3rd Jan 1998	Cardiff City	1	Oldham Athletic	0
3rd Jan 1998	Charlton Athletic	4	Nottingham Forest	1
4th Jan 1998	Chelsea	3	Manchester United	5
13th Jan 1998	Cheltenham Town	1	Reading	1
3rd Jan 1998	Crewe Alexandra	1	Birmingham City	2
3rd Jan 1998	Crystal Palace	2	Scunthorpe United	0
14th Jan 1998	Darlington	0	Wolverhampton Wands.	4
3rd Jan 1998	Derby County	2	Southampton	0
4th Jan 1998	Everton	0	Newcastle United	1
3rd Jan 1998	Grimsby Town	3	Norwich City	0
13th Jan 1998	Hereford United	0	Tranmere Rovers	3
3rd Jan 1998	Leeds United	4	Oxford United	0
3rd Jan 1998	Leicester City	4	Northampton Town	0
3rd Jan 1998	Liverpool	1	Coventry City	3
3rd Jan 1998	Manchester City	2	Bradford City	0
13th Jan 1998	Peterborough United	0	Walsall	2
3rd Jan 1998	Portsmouth	2	Aston Villa	2
3rd Jan 1998	Preston North End	1	Stockport County	2
3rd Jan 1998	Queen's Park Rangers	2	Middlesbrough	2
3rd Jan 1998	Rotherham United	1	Sunderland	5
3rd Jan 1998	Sheffield United	1	Bury	1
3rd Jan 1998	Swindon Town	1	Stevenage Borough	2

5th Jan 1998	Tottenham Hotspur 3	Fulham 1	
3rd Jan 1998	Watford 1	Sheffield Wednesday 1	
13th Jan 1998	West Bromwich Albion 3	Stoke City 1	
3rd Jan 1998	West Ham United 2	Emley 1	
4th Jan 1998	Wimbledon 0	Wrexham 0	

Replays

14th Jan 1998	Aston Villa 1	Portsmouth 0	
13th Jan 1998	Bury 1	Sheffield United 2	
13th Jan 1998	Ipswich Town 1	Bristol Rovers 0	
13th Jan 1998	Middlesbrough 2	Queen's Park Rangers 0	
14th Jan 1998	Port Vale 1	Arsenal 1	(aet)

Arsenal won 4-3 on penalties

20th Jan 1998	Reading 2	Cheltenham Town 1	
14th Jan 1998	Sheffield Wednesday 0	Watford 0	(aet)

Sheffield Wednesday won 5-3 on penalties

13th Jan 1998	Wrexham 2	Wimbledon 3	

Fourth Round

24th Jan 1998	Aston Villa 4	West Bromwich Albion 0	
24th Jan 1998	Birmingham City 2	Stockport County 1	
24th Jan 1998	Cardiff City 1	Reading 1	
24th Jan 1998	Charlton Athletic 1	Wolverhampton Wands. .. 1	
24th Jan 1998	Coventry City 2	Derby County 0	
24th Jan 1998	Crystal Palace 3	Leicester City 0	
24th Jan 1998	Huddersfield Town 0	Wimbledon 1	
24th Jan 1998	Ipswich Town 1	Sheffield United 1	
24th Jan 1998	Leeds United 2	Grimsby Town 0	
25th Jan 1998	Manchester City 1	West Ham United 2	
24th Jan 1998	Manchester United 5	Walsall 1	
24th Jan 1998	Middlesbrough 1	Arsenal 2	
26th Jan 1998	Sheffield Wednesday 0	Blackburn Rovers 3	
25th Jan 1998	Stevenage Borough 1	Newcastle United 1	
24th Jan 1998	Tottenham Hotspur 1	Barnsley 1	
24th Jan 1998	Tranmere Rovers 1	Sunderland 0	

Replays

4th Feb 1998	Barnsley 3	Tottenham Hotspur 1	
4th Feb 1998	Newcastle United 2	Stevenage Borough 1	
3rd Feb 1998	Reading 1	Cardiff City 1	(aet)

Reading won 4-3 on penalties

3rd Feb 1998	Sheffield United 1	Ipswich Town 0	
3rd Feb 1998	Wolverhampton Wands. .. 3	Charlton Athletic 0	

Fifth Round

15th Feb 1998	Arsenal	0	Crystal Palace	0
14th Feb 1998	Aston Villa	0	Coventry City	1
14th Feb 1998	Leeds United	3	Birmingham City	2
15th Feb 1998	Manchester United	1	Barnsley	1
14th Feb 1998	Newcastle United	1	Tranmere Rovers	0
13th Feb 1998	Sheffield United	1	Reading	0
14th Feb 1998	West Ham United	2	Blackburn Rovers	2
14th Feb 1998	Wimbledon	1	Wolverhampton Wands.	1

Replays

25th Feb 1998	Barnsley	3	Manchester United	2
25th Feb 1998	Blackburn Rovers	1	West Ham United	1 (aet)

West Ham United won 5-4 on penalties

25th Feb 1998	Crystal Palace	1	Arsenal	2
25th Feb 1998	Wolverhampton Wands.	2	Wimbledon	1

Sixth Round

8th Mar 1998	Arsenal	1	West Ham United	1
7th Mar 1998	Coventry City	1	Sheffield United	1
7th Mar 1998	Leeds United	0	Wolverhampton Wands.	1
8th Mar 1998	Newcastle United	3	Barnsley	1

Replays

17th Mar 1998	West Ham United	1	Arsenal	1 (aet)

Arsenal won 4-3 on penalties

17th Mar 1998	Sheffield United	1	Coventry City	1 (aet)

Sheffield United won 3-1 on penalties

Semi-Finals

6th Apr 1998	Sheffield United	0	Newcastle United	1
6th Apr 1998	Wolverhampton Wands.	0	Arsenal	1

FINAL

16th May 1998	Arsenal	2	Newcastle United	0

FOOTBALL LEAGUE CUP 1997/98

First Round (1st leg)

Date	Home		Away	
12th Aug 1997	Blackpool	1	Manchester City	0
12th Aug 1997	Bournemouth	0	Torquay United	1
12th Aug 1997	Brentford	1	Shrewsbury Town	1
13th Aug 1997	Brighton & Hove Albion	1	Leyton Orient	1
12th Aug 1997	Bristol City	0	Bristol Rovers	0
12th Aug 1997	Cambridge United	1	West Bromwich Albion	1
12th Aug 1997	Cardiff City	1	Southend United	1
13th Aug 1997	Charlton Athletic	0	Ipswich Town	1
12th Aug 1997	Chester City	1	Carlisle United	2
12th Aug 1997	Colchester United	0	Luton Town	1
12th Aug 1997	Crewe Alexandra	2	Bury	3
12th Aug 1997	Darlington	1	Notts County	1
11th Aug 1997	Doncaster Rovers	0	Nottingham Forest	8
12th Aug 1997	Gillingham	0	Birmingham City	1
12th Aug 1997	Huddersfield Town	2	Bradford City	1
12th Aug 1997	Lincoln City	1	Burnley	1
12th Aug 1997	Macclesfield Town	0	Hull City	0
12th Aug 1997	Mansfield Town	4	Stockport County	2
12th Aug 1997	Northampton Town	2	Millwall	1
12th Aug 1997	Norwich City	2	Barnet	1
12th Aug 1997	Oldham Athletic	1	Grimsby Town	0
12th Aug 1997	Oxford United	2	Plymouth Argyle	0
12th Aug 1997	Peterborough United	2	Portsmouth	2
12th Aug 1997	Port Vale	1	York City	2
12th Aug 1997	Queen's Park Rangers	0	Wolverhampton Wands.	2
12th Aug 1997	Reading	2	Swansea City	0
12th Aug 1997	Rochdale	1	Stoke City	3
12th Aug 1997	Rotherham United	1	Preston North End	3
12th Aug 1997	Scarborough	0	Scunthorpe United	2
13th Aug 1997	Swindon Town	0	Watford	2
12th Aug 1997	Tranmere Rovers	3	Hartlepool United	1
12th Aug 1997	Walsall	2	Exeter City	0
12th Aug 1997	Wigan Athletic	1	Chesterfield	2
12th Aug 1997	Wrexham	1	Sheffield United	1
12th Aug 1997	Wycombe Wanderers	1	Fulham	2

First Round (2nd leg)

26th Aug 1997   Barnet 3   Norwich City 1
Barnet won 4-3 on aggregate

26th Aug 1997   Birmingham City 3   Gillingham 0
Birmingham City won 4-0 on aggregate

26th Aug 1997   Bradford City 1   Huddersfield Town 1
Huddersfield Town won 3-2 on aggregate

26th Aug 1997   Bristol Rovers 1   Bristol City 2   (aet)
Bristol City won 2-1 on aggregate

26th Aug 1997   Burnley 2   Lincoln City 1
Burnley won 3-2 on aggregate

26th Aug 1997   Bury 3   Crewe Alexandra 3   (aet)
Bury won 6-5 on aggregate

26th Aug 1997   Carlisle United 3   Chester City 0
Carlisle United won 5-1 on aggregate

26th Aug 1997   Chesterfield 1   Wigan Athletic 0
Chesterfield won 3-1 on aggregate

26th Aug 1997   Exeter City 0   Walsall 1
Walsall won 3-0 on aggregate

26th Aug 1997   Fulham 4   Wycombe Wanderers 4
Fulham won 6-5 on aggregate

26th Aug 1997   Grimsby Town 5   Oldham Athletic 0
Grimsby Town won 5-1 on aggregate

26th Aug 1997   Hartlepool United 2   Tranmere Rovers 1
Tranmere Rovers won 4-3 on aggregate

26th Aug 1997   Hull City 2   Macclesfield Town 1   (aet)
Hull City won 2-1 on aggregate

26th Aug 1997   Ipswich Town 3   Charlton Athletic 1
Ipswich Town won 4-1 on aggregate

26th Aug 1997   Leyton Orient 3   Brighton & Hove Albion ... 1
Leyton Orient won 4-2 on aggregate

26th Aug 1997   Luton Town 1   Colchester United 1
Luton Town won 2-1 on aggregate

26th Aug 1997   Manchester City 1   Blackpool 0   (aet)
Aggregate score 1-1. Blackpool won 4-2 on penalties

27th Aug 1997   Millwall 2   Northampton Town 1   (aet)
Aggregate score 3-3. Millwall won 2-0 on penalties

First Round (2nd leg) continued

27th Aug 1997   Nottingham Forest 2   Doncaster Rovers 1
Nottingham Forest won 10-1 on aggregate

26th Aug 1997   Notts County 2   Darlington 1   (aet)
Notts County won 3-2 on aggregate

26th Aug 1997   Plymouth Argyle 3   Oxford United 5
Oxford United won 7-3 on aggregate

26th Aug 1997   Portsmouth 1   Peterborough 2
Peterborough United won 4-3 on aggregate

26th Aug 1997   Preston North End 2   Rotherham United 0
Preston North End won 5-1 on aggregate

26th Aug 1997   Scunthorpe United 2   Scarborough 1
Scunthorpe United won 4-1 on aggregate

26th Aug 1997   Sheffield United 3   Wrexham 1
Sheffield United won 4-2 on aggregate

26th Aug 1997   Shrewsbury Town 3   Brentford 5
Brentford won 6-4 on aggregate

26th Aug 1997   Southend United 3   Cardiff City 1
Southend United won 4-2 on aggregate

26th Aug 1997   Stockport County 6   Mansfield Town 3
Stockport County won 8-7 on aggregate

27th Aug 1997   Stoke City 1   Rochdale 1
Stoke City won 4-2 on aggregate

26th Aug 1997   Swansea City 1   Reading 1
Reading won 3-1 on aggregate

26th Aug 1997   Torquay United 1   Bournemouth 1   (aet)
Torquay United won 2-1 on aggregate

26th Aug 1997   Watford 1   Swindon Town 1
Watford won 3-1 on aggregate

27th Aug 1997   West Bromwich Albion 2   Cambridge United 1   (aet)
West Bromwich Albion won 3-2 on aggregate

27th Aug 1997   Wolverhampton Wands. .. 1   Queen's Park Rangers 2
Wolverhampton Wanderers won 3-2 on aggregate

26th Aug 1997   York City 1   Port Vale 1
York City won 3-2 on aggregate

Second Round (1st leg)

17th Sep 1997	Birmingham City	4	Stockport County	1
17th Sep 1997	Blackburn Rovers	6	Preston North End	0
17th Sep 1997	Grimsby Town	2	Sheffield Wednesday	0
17th Sep 1997	Leeds United	3	Bristol City	1
17th Sep 1997	Nottingham Forest	0	Walsall	1
17th Sep 1997	Southampton	3	Brentford	1
17th Sep 1997	Tottenham Hotspur	3	Carlisle United	2
16th Sep 1997	Blackpool	1	Coventry City	0
16th Sep 1997	Burnley	0	Stoke City	4
16th Sep 1997	Chesterfield	1	Barnsley	2
16th Sep 1997	Fulham	0	Wolverhampton Wands.	1
16th Sep 1997	Huddersfield Town	1	West Ham United	0
16th Sep 1997	Hull City	1	Crystal Palace	0
16th Sep 1997	Ipswich Town	1	Torquay United	1
16th Sep 1997	Leyton Orient	1	Bolton Wanderers	3
16th Sep 1997	Luton Town	1	West Bromwich Albion	1
16th Sep 1997	Middlesbrough	1	Barnet	0
16th Sep 1997	Notts County	0	Tranmere Rovers	2
16th Sep 1997	Oxford United	4	York City	1
16th Sep 1997	Reading	0	Peterborough United	0
16th Sep 1997	Scunthorpe United	0	Everton	1
16th Sep 1997	Southend United	0	Derby County	1
16th Sep 1997	Sunderland	2	Bury	1
16th Sep 1997	Watford	1	Sheffield United	1
16th Sep 1997	Wimbledon	5	Millwall	1

Second Round (2nd leg)

23rd Sep 1997	Barnet	0	Middlesbrough	2

Middlesbrough won 3-0 on aggregate

30th Sep 1997	Barnsley	4	Chesterfield	1

Barnsley won 6-2 on aggregate

30th Sep 1997	Bolton Wanderers	4	Leyton Orient	4

Bolton Wanderers won 7-5 on aggregate

30th Sep 1997	Brentford	0	Southampton	2

Southampton won 5-1 on aggregate

30th Sep 1997	Bristol City	2	Leeds United	1

Leeds United won 4-3 on aggregate

23rd Sep 1997	Bury	1	Sunderland	2

Sunderland won 4-2 on aggregate

30th Sep 1997   Carlisle United 0   Tottenham Hotspur 2
Tottenham Hotspur won 5-2 on aggregate

1st Oct 1997   Coventry City 3   Blackpool 1
Coventry City won 3-2 on aggregate

30th Sep 1997   Crystal Palace 2   Hull City 1
Aggregate score 2-2. Hull City won on the Away goals rule

1st Oct 1997   Derby County 5   Southend United 0
Derby County won 6-0 on aggregate

1st Oct 1997   Everton 5   Scunthorpe United 0
Everton won 6-0 on aggregate

1st Oct 1997   Millwall 1   Wimbledon 4
Wimbledon won 9-2 on aggregate

23rd Sep 1997   Peterborough United 0   Reading 2
Reading won 2-0 on aggregate

30th Sep 1997   Preston North End 1   Blackburn Rovers 0
Blackburn Rovers won 6-1 on aggregate

23rd Sep 1997   Sheffield United 4   Watford 0
Sheffield United won 5-1 on aggregate

1st Oct 1997   Sheffield Wednesday 3   Grimsby Town 2
Grimsby Town won 4-3 on aggregate

23rd Sep 1997   Stockport County 2   Birmingham City 1
Birmingham City won 5-3 on aggregate

24th Sep 1997   Stoke City 2   Burnley 0
Stoke City won 6-0 on aggregate

23rd Sep 1997   Torquay United 0   Ipswich Town 3
Ipswich Town won 4-1 on aggregate

23rd Sep 1997   Tranmere Rovers 0   Notts County 1
Tranmere Rovers won 2-1 on aggregate

24th Sep 1997   Walsall 2   Nottingham Forest 2   (aet)
Walsall won 3-2 on aggregate

23rd Sep 1997   West Bromwich Albion 4   Luton Town 2
West Bromwich Albion won 5-3 on aggregate

29th Sep 1997   West Ham United 3   Huddersfield Town 0
West Ham United won 3-1 on aggregate

24th Sep 1997   Wolverhampton Wands. .. 1   Fulham 0
Wolverhampton Wanderers won 2-0 on aggregate

23rd Sep 1997   York City 1   Oxford United 2
Oxford United won 6-1 on aggregate

Third Round

14th Oct 1997	Arsenal	4	Birmingham City	1	
14th Oct 1997	Barnsley	1	Southampton	2	
14th Oct 1997	Bolton Wanderers	2	Wimbledon	0	(aet)
14th Oct 1997	Grimsby Town	3	Leicester City	1	
14th Oct 1997	Ipswich Town	2	Manchester United	0	
14th Oct 1997	Oxford United	1	Tranmere Rovers	1	(aet)

Oxford United won 6-5 on penalties

14th Oct 1997	Reading	4	Wolverhampton Wands.	2	
14th Oct 1997	Walsall	2	Sheffield United	1	
15th Oct 1997	Chelsea	1	Blackburn Rovers	1	(aet)

Chelsea won 4-1 on penalties

15th Oct 1997	Coventry City	4	Everton	1	
15th Oct 1997	Middlesbrough	2	Sunderland	0	
15th Oct 1997	Newcastle United	2	Hull City	0	
15th Oct 1997	Stoke City	1	Leeds United	3	(aet)
15th Oct 1997	Tottenham Hotspur	1	Derby County	2	
15th Oct 1997	West Bromwich Albion	0	Liverpool	2	
15th Oct 1997	West Ham United	3	Aston Villa	0	

Fourth Round

18th Nov 1997	Derby County	0	Newcastle United	1	
18th Nov 1997	Liverpool	3	Grimsby Town	0	
18th Nov 1997	Leeds United	2	Reading	3	
18th Nov 1997	Oxford United	1	Ipswich Town	2	(aet)
19th Nov 1997	West Ham United	4	Walsall	1	
18th Nov 1997	Arsenal	1	Coventry City	0	(aet)
18th Nov 1997	Middlesbrough	2	Bolton Wanderers	1	(aet)
19th Nov 1997	Chelsea	2	Southampton	1	(aet)

Fifth Round

6th Jan 1998	Reading	0	Middlesbrough	1	
6th Jan 1998	West Ham United	1	Arsenal	2	
7th Jan 1998	Ipswich Town	2	Chelsea	2	(aet)

Chelsea won 4-1 on penalties

7th Jan 1998	Newcastle United	0	Liverpool	2	(aet)

Semi-Finals (1st leg)

27th Jan 1998   Liverpool 2   Middlesbrough 1

28th Jan 1998   Arsenal 2   Chelsea 1

Semi-Finals (2nd leg)

18th Feb 1998   Middlesbrough 2   Liverpool 0

Middlesbrough won 3-2 on aggregate

18th Feb 1998   Chelsea 3   Arsenal 1

Chelsea won 4-3 on aggregate

FINAL

29th Mar 1998   Chelsea 2   Middlesbrough 0

ENGLAND INTERNATIONAL LINE-UPS AND STATISTICS 1997-98

10th September 1997
MOLDOVA (WCQ) *Wembley*

Seaman	Arsenal
G. Neville	Manchester United
P. Neville	Manchester United
Batty	Newcastle United
Campbell	Tottenham Hotspur
Southgate	Aston Villa
Beckham	Manchester United (sub. Ripley)
(sub. Butt))	
Gascoigne	Glasgow Rangers
Ferdinand	Tottenham Hotspur (sub. Collymore)
Wright	Arsenal
Scholes	Manchester United

Result 4-0 Scholes, Wright 2, Gascoigne

11th October 1997
ITALY (WCQ) *Rome*

Seaman	Arsenal
Campbell	Tottenham Hotspur
Le Saux	Chelsea
Ince	Liverpool
Adams	Arsenal
Southgate	Aston Villa
Beckham	Manchester United
Gascoigne	Glasgow Rangers (sub. Butt)
Wright	Arsenal
Sheringham	Manchester United
Batty	Newcastle United

Result 0-0

15th November 1997
CAMEROON *Wembley*

Martyn	Leeds United
Campbell	Tottenham Hotspur
G. Neville	Manchester United
Ince	Liverpool
Southgate	Aston Villa (sub. R. Ferdinand)
Hinchcliffe	Everton
Beckham	Manchester United
Gascoigne	Glasgow Rangers (sub. Lee)
Fowler	Liverpool
Scholes	Manchester Utd (sub. Sutton)
McManaman	Liverpool

Result 2-0 Fowler, Scholes

11th February 1998
CHILE *Wembley*

Martyn	Leeds United
G. Neville	Manchester United
Campbell	Tottenham Hotspur
Batty	Newcastle United (sub. Ince)
Adams	Arsenal
P. Neville	Manchester U. (sub. Le Saux)
Lee	Newcastle United
Butt	Manchester United
Dublin	Coventry City
Sheringham	Manchester U. (sub. Shearer)
Owen	Liverpool

Result 0-2

25th March 1998
SWITZERLAND *Berne*

Flowers	Blackburn Rovers
Keown	Arsenal
Hinchcliffe	Everton
R. Ferdinand	West Ham United
Southgate	Aston Villa
Ince	Liverpool
Merson	Middlesbrough (sub. Batty)
McManaman	Liverpool
Shearer	Newcastle United
Owen	Liverpool (sub. Sheringham)
Lee	Newcastle United

Result 1-1 Merson

22nd April 1998
PORTUGAL *Wembley*

Seaman	Arsenal
G. Neville	Manchester Utd. (sub. P. Neville)
Le Saux	Chelsea
Ince	Liverpool
Adams	Arsenal
Campbell	Tottenham Hotspur
Beckham	Manchester U. (sub. Merson)
Batty	Newcastle United
Shearer	Newcastle United
Sheringham	Manchester Utd. (sub. Owen)
Scholes	Manchester United

Result 3-0 Shearer 2, Sheringham

ENGLAND INTERNATIONAL LINE-UPS AND STATISTICS 1998

23rd May 1998
SAUDI ARABIA *Wembley*

Seaman	Arsenal
Seaman	Arsenal
G. Neville	Manchester United
Hinchcliffe	Everton (sub. P. Neville)
Batty	Newcastle United
Adams	Arsenal
Southgate	Aston Villa
Beckham	Manchester U. (sub. Gascoigne)
Anderton	Tottenham Hotspur
Shearer	Newcastle U. (sub. L. Ferdinand)
Sheringham	Manchester United (sub. Wright)
Scholes	Manchester United

Result 0-0

27th May 1998
v MOROCCO *Casablanca*

Flowers	Blackburn Rovers
Keown	Arsenal
Le Saux	Chelsea
Ince	Liverpool
Campbell	Tottenham Hotspur
Southgate	Aston Villa
Anderton	Tottenham Hotspur
Gascoigne	Middlesbrough
Dublin	Coventry City (sub L. Ferdinand)
Wright	Arsenal (sub Owen)
McManaman	Liverpool

Result 1-0 Owen

29th May 1998
v BELGIUM *Casablanca*

Martyn	Leeds United
G. Neville	Manchester Utd. (sub. R. Ferdinand)
P. Neville	Manchester Utd. (sub. Owen)
Butt	Manchester United
Campbell	Tottenham Hotspur (sub. Dublin)
Keown	Arsenal
Lee	Newcastle United
Gascoigne	Middlesbrough (sub. Beckham)
L. Ferdinand	Tottenham Hotspur
Merson	Middlesbrough
Le Saux	Chelsea

Result 0-0
Belgium won 4-3 on penalties

15th June 1998
v TUNISIA (WC) *Marseille*

Seaman	Arsenal
Campbell	Tottenham Hotspur
Le Saux	Chelsea
Adams	Arsenal
Southgate	Aston Villa
Ince	Liverpool
Batty	Newcastle United
Scholes	Manchester United
Anderton	Tottenham Hotspur
Shearer	Newcastle United
Sheringham	Manchester Utd. (sub. Owen)

Result 2-0 Shearer, Scholes

22nd June 1998
v ROMANIA (WC) *Montpellier*

Seaman	Arsenal
Adams	Arsenal
Campbell	Tottenham Hotspur
Le Saux	Chelsea
G. Neville	Manchester United
Anderton	Tottenham Hotspur
Batty	Newcastle United
Ince	Liverpool (sub. Beckham)
Scholes	Manchester United
Shearer	Newcastle United
Sheringham	Manchester Utd. (sub. Owen)

Result 1-2 Owen

26th June 1998
v COLOMBIA (WC) *Lens*

Seaman	Arsenal
G. Neville	Manchester United
Adams	Arsenal
Campbell	Tottenham Hotspur
Anderton	Tottenham Hotspur (sub. Lee)
Le Saux	Chelsea
Ince	Liverpool (sub. Batty)
Scholes	Manchester Utd. (sub. McManaman)
Beckham	Manchester United
Owen	Liverpool
Shearer	Newcastle United

Result 2-0 Anderton, Beckham

30th June 1998
v ARGENTINA (WC) *Saint-Etienne*
Seaman   Arsenal
Campbell   Tottenham Hotspur
Le Saux   Chelsea (sub. Southgate)
Adams   Arsenal
G. Neville   Manchester United
Ince   Liverpool
Beckham   Manchester United
Anderton   Tottenham Hotspur (sub. Batty)
Scholes   Manchester Utd. (sub. Merson)
Shearer   Newcastle United
Owen   Liverpool
Result 2-2 Shearer (pen), Owen
After extra time, Argentina won 4-3 on penalties

THE INTERNATIONAL LINE-UPS & STATISTICS SERIES

This series of A5-sized handbooks provides a match-by-match record of each country's international matches. Each book includes dates, opponents, venues, team line-ups, substitutes used, scores and scorers.

TITLES AVAILABLE: –

Argentina 1902-1970	*Argentina 1970-1997*
Brazil 1914-1970	*Brazil 1971-1996*
Canada 1885-1995	*Colombia 1938-1996*
Ecuador 1938-1997	*Eire 1921-1996*
England 1872-1960	*England 1961-1996*
Israel 1934-1995	*New Zealand 1885-1995*
Northern Ireland 1882-1997	*Paraguay 1919-1996*
Peru 1927-1996	*Scotland 1872-1960*
U.S.A. 1885-1995	*Wales 1876-1960*

Wales 1961-1996

Olympic Football 1900-1964   *Olympic Football 1968-96*

Order from Soccer Books Limited
Price of each book £5.95 – surface postage free

The Supporters' Guide Series

This top-selling series has been published annually since 1982 and contains: – 1997/98 Season's results and tables; Directions; Ground plans; Photos; Phone numbers; Parking information; Admission details; Disabled information and much more.

THE SUPPORTERS' GUIDE TO PREMIER & FOOTBALL LEAGUE CLUBS 1999

The 15th edition featuring all Premiership and Football League clubs.   *Price £5.99*

THE SUPPORTERS' GUIDE TO NON-LEAGUE FOOTBALL 1999

The 7th edition featuring all Conference, Unibond Premier, Rymans Premier and Dr. Martens Premier clubs.   *Price £5.99*

THE SUPPORTERS' GUIDE TO SCOTTISH FOOTBALL 1999

The 7th edition featuring all Scottish League and Highland League clubs.   *Price £5.99*

THE SUPPORTERS' GUIDE TO WELSH FOOTBALL 1998

The 5th edition featuring all League of Wales, Cymru Alliance & Welsh Football League Clubs.   *Price £4.99*

THE SUPPORTERS' GUIDE TO IRISH FOOTBALL 1998

2nd edition featuring all Smirnoff Premier & 1st Division Irish League clubs, all FAI Harp Lager National League clubs plus Wilkinson Sword Irish League 'B' Division clubs.   *Price £4.99*

THE SUPPORTERS' GUIDE TO FOOTBALL PROGRAMMES 1998

The 3rd edition featuring information on the Programmes of all Premiership and Football League clubs.   *Price £4.99*

All books priced as above and available post free – Order from:

Soccer Books Limited (Dept. SBL)
72 St. Peter's Avenue
Cleethorpes
N.E. Lincolnshire
DN35 8HU

SOCCER BOOKS LIMITED
72 ST. PETER'S AVENUE
CLEETHORPES
N.E. LINCOLNSHIRE
DN35 8HU

Phone (01472) 696226
Fax (01472) 698546

Web site: http://www.soccer-books.co.uk
e-mail: info@soccbook.demon.co.uk

BACK NUMBERS

We still have the undermentioned publications available post free at the prices shown. There are very few remaining copies of some of these titles so, please, order any that you require without delay to avoid disappointment.

Year	TITLE	Price	Qty	Order Value
1990	The Supporters' Guide to Football League Clubs 1991	£3.95		
1991	The Supporters' Guide to Football League Clubs 1992	£4.99		
1993	The Supporters' Gd. to Premier & Football League Clubs 1994	£4.99		
1993	The Supporters' Guide to Non-League Football 1994	£4.99		
1993	The Supporters' Guide to Welsh Football 1994	£4.99		
1994	The Supporters' Gd. to Premier & Football League Clubs 1995	£4.99		
1994	The Supporters' Guide to Scottish Football 1995	£4.99		
1994	The Supporters' Guide to Non-League Football 1995	£4.99		
1994	The Supporters' Guide to Welsh Football 1995	£4.99		
1995	The Supporters' Gd. to Premier & Football League Clubs 1996	£4.99		
1995	The Supporters' Guide to Scottish Football 1996	£4.99		
1995	The Supporters' Guide to Non-League Football 1996	£4.99		
1995	The Supporters' Guide to Welsh Football 1996	£4.99		
1995	The Supporters' Guide to Football Programmes 1996	£4.99		
1996	The Supp. Guide to Premiership & Football League Clubs 1997	£4.99		
1996	The Supporters' Guide to Scottish Football 1997	£4.99		
1996	The Supporters' Guide to Non-League Football 1997	£4.99		
1996	The Supporters' Guide to Welsh Football 1997	£4.99		
1996	The Supporters' Guide to Irish Football 1997	£4.99		
1996	The Supporters' Guide to Football Programmes 1997	£4.99		
1997	The Supporters' Gd. to Premier & Football League Clubs 1998	£4.99		
1997	The Supporters' Guide to Scottish Football 1998	£4.99		
1997	The Supporters' Guide to Non-League Football 1998	£4.99		

What the grounds really look like : –

PREMIERSHIP AND 1ST DIVISION FOOTBALL GROUNDS BEFORE AND AFTER TAYLOR

Featuring 4 postcard-size full-colour photographs of views from the stands of each of the 44 Premiership and 1st Division clubs (1995/96 Season).

2 photos for each club from 1990/91 and 1995/96.

Printed on high quality art paper.

SOFTBACK PRICE £9.99

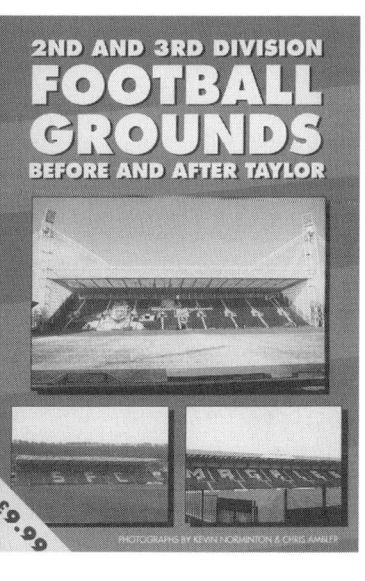

2ND AND 3RD DIVISION FOOTBALL GROUNDS BEFORE AND AFTER TAYLOR

Featuring 4 postcard-size full-colour photographs of views from the stands of each of the 48 2nd and 3rd Division clubs (1995/96 Season).

2 photos for each club from 1990/91 and 1995/96.

Printed on high quality art paper.

SOFTBACK PRICE £9.99

Postage per book:
UK – FREE • Overseas £1.50 • Airmail £4.00

Available from your local bookshop or directly from:

Soccer Books Limited (Dept. SBL)
72 St. Peter's Avenue
Cleethorpes
N.E. Lincolnshire
DN35 8HU
Tel. (01472) 696226   Fax (01472) 698546

**SPECIAL OFFER —
ORDER BOTH BOOKS
DIRECTLY FOR JUST**

£15.00

(surface post free)

SOCCER BOOKS LIMITED

72 ST. PETERS AVENUE (Dept. SBL)
CLEETHORPES
N.E. LINCOLNSHIRE
DN35 8HU
ENGLAND
Tel. 01472 696226/601893   Fax 01472 698546

Web site http://www.soccer-books.co.uk
e-mail info@soccbook.demon.co.uk

Established in 1982, Soccer Books Limited has now combined its book/video selling business (TH
SOCCER BOOKSHELF) with its publishing business (SOCCER BOOK PUBLISHING LIMITED
under a single company, to streamline the processing of orders.

Already the suppliers of the biggest range of English-Language soccer books and videos, we are no
expanding our stocks even further to include many more titles including German, French, Spanis
and Italian-language books.

With over 100,000 satisfied customers already, we supply books to virtually every country in th
world but have maintained the friendliness and accessibility associated with a small family-ru
business. The range of titles we sell includes:

YEARBOOKS – All major yearbooks including Rothmans (12 editions), Calcios (8 editions
Supporters' Guides (6 editions + back numbers), F.A. Yearbooks (3 editions), Playfair Annuals (
editions), Northern Ireland Yearbooks (3 editions), North & Latin American Guides (3 editions
African Guides, Sky Sports Guides, Non-League Directories.

CLUB HISTORIES – Complete Records (18 clubs), Official Histories (20 titles), 25 Year Record
(21 clubs), Definitive Histories (8 clubs) plus many more including books on German clubs.

WORLD FOOTBALL – World Cup books (20 titles), International Line-up & Statistics Series (1
titles), European Championships History, Guinness Book of World Soccer, International League
Club Histories (46 titles) and much more.

BIOGRAPHIES & WHO'S WHOS – Managers: Dalglish, Ferguson, Venables, Paisley, Shank
Busby and others; Players: Dicks, Trautmann, Rush, Cantona, Ginola and others; Who's Who
Guinness and others – including clubs.

ENCYCLOPEDIAS & GENERAL TITLES – Football Grounds of Britain, Hooligan studies, Histor
of the F.A. Cup, History of the Wembley Cup Final and dozens of others.

VIDEOS – Season's highlights, histories, big games, World Cup, European Championships, play
profiles, F.A. Cup Finals – including many back items.

For a current listing of our titles, please contact us using the information at the top of the page.

THE 25 YEAR RECORD SERIES

Top quality 25 Season histories with line-ups, results, scorers, attendances and season-by-season write-ups.

Titles currently available:

Hearts	Seasons 1973-74 to 1997-98
Manchester City F.C.	Seasons 1973-74 to 1997-98
Watford F.C.	Seasons 1973-74 to 1997-98
West Ham United F.C.	Seasons 1973-74 to 1997-98
Arsenal F.C.	Seasons 1972-73 to 1996-97
Crystal Palace F.C.	Seasons 1972-73 to 1996-97
Spurs	Seasons 1972-73 to 1996-97
West Bromwich Albion F.C.	Seasons 1972-73 to 1996-97
Wolves	Seasons 1972-73 to 1996-97
Chelsea F.C.	Seasons 1971-72 to 1995-96
Middlesbrough F.C.	Seasons 1971-72 to 1995-96
Preston North End F.C.	Seasons 1971-72 to 1995-96
Southampton F.C.	Seasons 1971-72 to 1995-96
Sunderland F.C.	Seasons 1971-72 to 1995-96
Aston Villa F.C.	Seasons 1970-71 to 1994-95
Celtic F.C.	Seasons 1970-71 to 1994-95
Derby County F.C.	Seasons 1970-71 to 1994-95
Everton F.C.	Seasons 1970-71 to 1994-95
Leeds United F.C.	Seasons 1970-71 to 1994-95
Liverpool F.C.	Seasons 1970-71 to 1994-95
Manchester United F.C.	Seasons 1970-71 to 1994-95
Newcastle United F.C.	Seasons 1970-71 to 1994-95
Nottingham Forest F.C.	Seasons 1970-71 to 1994-95
Rangers F.C.	Seasons 1970-71 to 1994-95

Also available (no write-ups):

Burnley F.C.	Seasons 1969-70 to 1993-94

All titles are softback and priced £4.99

Available post free from:

Soccer Books Limited (Dept. SBL)
72 St. Peter's Avenue
Cleethorpes
N.E. Lincolnshire
DN35 8HU

Tel: (01472) 696226
Fax: (01472) 698546